the
LEADING EDUCATOR
S E R I E S

Improbable Probabilities

The Unlikely Journey of Yong Zhao

G. WILLIAMSON MCDIARMID

YONG ZHAO

Solution Tree | Press
a division of
Solution Tree

555 North Morton Street
Bloomington, IN 47404
800.733.6786 (toll free) / 812.336.7700
FAX: 812.336.7790
email: info@SolutionTree.com
SolutionTree.com

Printed in the United States of America

Library of Congress Cataloging-in-Publication Data

Names: 880-01 Zhao, Yong (Writer on education), author. | McDiarmid, G.
    Williamson, author.
Title: Improbable probabilities : the unlikely journey of Yong Zhao / Yong
    Zhao, G. Williamson McDiarmid.
Description: Bloomington : Solution Tree Press, [2022] | Includes
    bibliographical references and index.
Identifiers: LCCN 2022017176 (print) | LCCN 2022017177 (ebook) | ISBN
    9781952812415 (Hardcover) | ISBN 9781952812422 (eBook)
Subjects: LCSH: 880-06 Zhao, Yong (Writer on education) |
    Educators--China--20th century--Biography.
Classification: LCC LA2383.C52 Z4738 2022 (print) | LCC LA2383.C52
    (ebook) | DDC 370.92 [B]--dc23/eng/20220824
LC record available at https://lccn.loc.gov/2022017176
LC ebook record available at https://lccn.loc.gov/2022017177

Solution Tree
Jeffrey C. Jones, CEO
Edmund M. Ackerman, President

Solution Tree Press
President and Publisher: Douglas M. Rife
Associate Publisher: Sarah Payne-Mills
Managing Production Editor: Kendra Slayton
Editorial Director: Todd Brakke
Art Director: Rian Anderson
Copy Chief: Jessi Finn
Production Editor: Paige Duke
Content Development Specialist: Amy Rubenstein
Copy Editor: Madonna Evans
Proofreader: Sarah Ludwig
Text and Cover Designer: Kelsey Hoover
Associate Editor: Sarah Ludwig
Editorial Assistants: Charlotte Jones and Elijah Oates

This book is dedicated to Yong's parents,
who gave him the greatest of all gifts—
the freedom to be himself.

Acknowledgments

I t is impossible to list all the people who have contributed significantly to Yong's life, and only a few appear by name in this book. These people, intentionally or not, created opportunities for Yong to discover, develop, and make use of his passions and talents. They provided advice, support, and challenges on Yong's journey. Without them, Yong's life would be very different and a book like this might not have been written. Yong is, thus, forever grateful for them and their appearances at the right time and place in his life.

Though they may never read this book, Yong acknowledges the people in his village in Sichuan Province for the ways in which they shaped his early life: tolerating his unconventional behaviors and ideas, enjoying his peculiar habit of telling stories from his reading and his imagination, allowing him to be himself instead of ridiculing him for being different, and treating him kindly despite his unconventional path.

Yong is forever grateful to his teachers for their generosity, kindness, and tolerance—those essential elements of the environment that shaped him to become the person he is today. He had a wonderful time in school, where he found a sanctuary for his uncommon thoughts and behaviors.

During his time at the Sichuan Foreign Language Institute, today's Sichuan International Studies University, Yong read broadly, interacted with international teachers, and discovered his passions and abilities. He is deeply thankful to his colleagues across the institute, and especially those in the Teacher Education Department, for their openness, warmth, and motivation. They provided a stimulating and productive dynamic for his growth. In particular, he would like to thank Professor Bi Zhao, who introduced him to pedagogical studies and allowed him to work on the Chopsticks Circle Study, and Professor Weiming Zhang, dean of the Teacher Education Program, who launched the computer course that inspired Yong's interest in technology.

Thanks to Keith Campbell, who was instrumental in bringing Yong to Linfield College—the first American educational institute he visited—and who provided him with opportunities to live and work there. Thanks also to other colleagues and staff in the Linfield Department of Education who gave him opportunities to teach and work with the internet, a new technology at the time.

Yong's experiences at the University of Illinois Urbana-Champaign were transformative. He had access to invigorating courses, the emerging internet, a rich library, and opportunities for graduate assistantships. Yong is particularly indebted to Gary Cziko, his academic advisor, who gave him maximum freedom, encouraged him to explore, and guided him toward new theories and possibilities in education. Yong is also indebted to David Zola, who hired him as a teaching assistant for the most popular course in educational psychology on campus, which enabled him to learn a great deal about teaching American students at a large university.

Yong would like to express his thanks for the fifteen years he spent at the College of Education at Michigan State University (MSU), where he found opportunities to grow professionally and learn from many amazing scholars with expansive expertise and aspirations. Of his many supporters at MSU, Yong wants to thank in particular Dean Carole Ames and Department Chair Dick Prawat for their support and encouragement. Thanks also to Professor Penelope Peterson for the opportunity to develop the American Educational Research Association (AERA) submission portal project, Professor Patrick Dickson for challenging and inspirational conversations about educational technology, Professors Punya Mishra and Ken Frank for their wonderful collaborations and friendships, Barbara Markle for the many opportunities to work in Michigan public schools, and Professor Jack Schwille for the encouragement to explore work internationally.

Yong is also grateful for his five years at the University of Oregon, where he met many extraordinary people who helped shape his thinking about education. The most important influence was Ron Beghetto, who is now a distinguished professor at Arizona State University. Yong is forever thankful for his beautiful collaborations and excellent conversations with Ron.

The University of Kansas, where Yong works now, has offered Yong the opportunity to explore broad and significant issues in education. He is deeply indebted to Dean Rick Ginsberg, who has provided support and opportunities and has been an engaging collaborator in writing and thinking. Thanks also to Jim Watterston, dean of the Melbourne Graduate School of Education, for the opportunity to teach in Australia and to collaborate in writing.

Additionally, several scholars' works have had a profound impact on Yong's thinking. While still living in China, Yong read Thomas Good and Jere Brophy's co-authored *Educational Psychology*, which greatly impacted his early thinking about education. Other important books that influenced Yong's thinking are David Berliner and Bruce Biddle's *The Manufactured Crisis* and Stephen Jay Gould's *The Mismeasure of Man*.

The danger in attempting to identify all the people who have supported and encouraged Yong on his journey is that any listing will be incomplete. A full accounting would require an entire chapter, not just a couple of pages. These people are as integral to his life and contributions as are those identified above. He wishes to also acknowledge and thank these unnamed but not unappreciated individuals.

Finally, Yong would like to thank his family for their love, support, and tolerance!

Bill would similarly like to thank Robin Rogers, his tolerant and supportive spouse, who read early drafts and offered helpful observations and advice. Cap Peck read an early chapter draft and asked a question that Bill and Yong returned to frequently in writing the book: "What is this a case of?" This gave rise to the book's introduction and prompted us to use Richard Lewontin's triple helix to frame Yong's story.

Finally, we wish to acknowledge our editor at Solution Tree, Paige Duke. Her questions, suggestions, and careful and thoughtful editing were invaluable. Thank you, Paige.

Contents

About the Authors

Yong Zhao, PhD, is foundation distinguished professor of education at the University of Kansas, and professor of educational leadership at the Melbourne Graduate School of Education, Australia. Yong was presidential chair and director of the Institute for Global and Online Education in the College of Education at the University of Oregon and a professor in the Department of Educational Measurement, Policy, and Leadership. He was previously university distinguished professor in the College of Education at Michigan State University, where he was founding director of the Office of Teaching and Technology and the U.S.-China Center for Research on Educational Excellence, and executive director of the Confucius Institute. He is an elected member of the National Academy of Education and elected fellow of the International Academy of Education.

Yong is an internationally known scholar, author, and speaker whose works focus on the implications of globalization and technology on education. He has designed schools that cultivate global competence, developed computer games for language learning, and founded research and development institutions to explore innovative education models. The author of more than one hundred articles and thirty books, he was named one of the ten most influential people in educational technology in 2012 by the magazine *Tech & Learning*.

Yong received a bachelor of arts degree in English language education from the Sichuan Foreign Language Institute in Chongqing, China, and a master of arts and doctorate in education from the University of Illinois Urbana-Champaign.

G. Williamson McDiarmid is the former dean and alumni distinguished professor emeritus at the University of North Carolina at Chapel Hill, and distinguished chair of education at East China Normal University in Shanghai, China.

Preface

February 2022
Eugene, Oregon

Everyone is born with a probability for their future. Birth locations, family circumstances, and community resources shape the likelihood of a particular life in the future.[1] For instance, a person born in a remote rural area is much less likely to work on Wall Street than a person born in a wealthy suburb of a big city. Similarly, a person born into a family with illiterate parents is much less likely to become a white-collar worker than a person born into a family with parents who hold doctoral degrees.[2]

But probability is a *likelihood*—it is not a certainty. People born into disadvantaged families are not destined to fare worse than those born into advantaged families. Children from poor families can defy probability and enter worlds typically dominated by those born with more resources. Despite many initiatives to level the playing field for all children—such as Head Start, Child First, the Perry Preschool Project, and the Abecedarian Project, to name a few[3]—the reality is the divide between the haves and have-nots has grown.[4] Education, the social tool many believe has the greatest power to equalize opportunities across social classes, has failed to do so for many students. Family income and parental background are still the most significant determiners of student achievement. Associate Professor Anna Chmielewski conducted a meta-analysis of thirty major research studies on the socioeconomic achievement gap and concluded that there is "strong and robust evidence of increasing SES [socioeconomic status] achievement gaps over the past 50 years across the majority of countries examined."[5] Societies should continue to strive for social, political, and socioeconomic equity with the goal of leveling the playing field for children everywhere, and teachers must work with students to improve the probabilities that their lives will be fulfilling and contributive. Evidence suggests that, despite the odds, education can change students' life chances.[6] Probabilities are not destiny—as my story illustrates. This book describes how I managed to defy the probabilities into which I was born.

Given the circumstances of my birth, the probability that I would become a professor in the United States was roughly equal to the probability that I would win a Powerball jackpot. I was born into a family with two illiterate parents and three illiterate or semi-illiterate sisters in a small, remote rural village in China in 1965. I grew up in a China that was wracked by two major historical events: the Great Leap Forward and the Great Cultural Revolution.

HISTORICAL CONTEXT

Chinese Communist Party (CCP) Chairman Mao Zedong initiated the Great Leap Forward (1958-1962), hoping to transform China into a Communist paradise and accelerate industrialization by creating large-scale rural communes.[7] Not only was the initiative unsuccessful, but it also backfired. Due to hasty implementation, natural calamities, and economic breakdown, an estimated twenty million people died of starvation.[8]

Four years later, Chairman Mao initiated the Great Proletarian Cultural Revolution (1966-1976), intending to purify the ranks of the Communist Party.[9] The period was marked by social chaos as gangs of students and Red Guards—student-led paramilitary

groups devoted to carrying out Mao's new program—
mobilized and attacked people who wore bourgeois
clothes, tore down imperialist signs, and murdered
intellectuals and Party officials.[10] This decade of violence,
turmoil, and bloodshed was responsible for the
deaths of nearly two million people, displaced millions
more, and completely disrupted China's economy.[11]

During this turmoil, China was isolated from the rest of the
world. The imperialist United States was the number one enemy.
The extreme remoteness of our village insulated us somewhat from
the social and political turmoil that roiled urban areas during the
Cultural Revolution. However, the devastating malnutrition and
near starvation that tens of millions of Chinese suffered in the wake
of the disastrous Great Leap Forward were commonplace in my village. Some days, we had only a thin broth made from a handful of
rice and a few sweet potato slices; on other days, we had to make
do with only the potato slices. Acute and constant hunger was the
norm. As children, we were so accustomed to hunger that it didn't
warrant discussion.

Despite the odds against me, I have worked as a professor at multiple universities in the United States and Australia since 1996. In
so doing, I have defied the high probability of becoming another
peasant farmer in China. My journey of defying probability is both
random and complicated, involving interactions between me and
my environment. The journey is replete with chance occurrences and
unexpected events. Unforeseen meetings with talented and generous
people influenced me greatly. My life seems ordinary in many ways,
but in other ways is exceptional. From the day-to-day perspective,
it seems normal, but over the scope of a lifetime, it appears highly
improbable.

How did I defy the probabilities that were my birthright? A conventional answer would be that I was exceptionally bright or talented. However, that is not true. I am no more intelligent or talented than my younger brother who became a truck driver. Another answer would be that I was just luckier than others in my village. Yet, no one in my village got lucky breaks, including my family members.

No single factor defined how my life unfolded. I hope that analyzing my life, as this book attempts to do, can identify some of the factors that helped me defy the probabilities into which I was born. Although each person is unique, some universal themes can be drawn from our experiences. This book highlights the possibility of transcending probabilities assigned at birth as one such theme. Thus, I treat this memoir as a case study of the myriad factors that help people beat their probabilities. Although this is my story, I view my journey as a data set from which we can extract lessons that will be helpful to teachers, parents, and students. This requires viewing all children as capable of maximizing their potential, regardless of the circumstances into which they are born. Rather than assuming children have predefined and limited possibilities, supporting them as they explore, experiment, mind-wander, and find their own paths increases the likelihood that they will discover unforeseen opportunities that will allow them to defy their probabilities.

As I considered how to approach my story, I realized it would benefit from a second perspective: I needed a collaborator. Such a collaborator would likely find significance in particular events or happenings that I might overlook. To borrow a phrase from art and anthropology, I needed someone who, in exploring my life, could make the familiar strange.

The collaborator, I reasoned, should be someone who was born and raised in the United States and, thus, would tell my story from a Western perspective. The collaborator should also be someone with a great deal of global experience so my story can be analyzed from both a global and local viewpoint. I needed someone who had a grasp of modern Chinese history and Chinese education. More broadly, the collaborator should be an expert in educational research and thoroughly understand educational contexts and policies.

I was fortunate to find Professor G. Williamson McDiarmid (better known as Bill), former dean of the School of Education at the University of North Carolina at Chapel Hill and alumni distinguished professor emeritus. Bill is a North Carolina native with an abiding connection to his family's farm. In many ways, his life is similar to mine. He was born with little probability of becoming an accomplished scholar. He has lived and worked in different parts of the world, including Greece, Pakistan, and China, and has traveled throughout Europe, East Africa, and the Middle East. Bill is also a seasoned researcher with a solid grasp of educational issues. We originally met in passing at Michigan State University in 1996, and then again at East China Normal University in Shanghai in 2017. After we teamed up to write *Learning for Uncertainty*, I knew I'd found my collaborator.[12]

Bill and I worked on this book for more than a year. We had weekly Zoom meetings, in which we talked about my life, educational issues in various countries, and the potential lessons my story offered that could help people defy their probabilities. After asking many questions to probe certain happenings or my thinking during past events, Bill completed the writing. He also researched the historical context as well as the analytical concepts we use to understand my story. I then read his drafts and made revisions that we discussed in subsequent Zoom meetings.

As I'd hoped, this approach allowed me to examine my life through a more global and dispassionate lens. Sometimes a shift in perspective is exactly what we need to notice the significance of past events; an outside observer helps us to make the familiar strange. While this book tells my story, it is a co-construction. Had I written it by myself, I am not sure it would have the same appeal, nor would it have likely unpacked so many of my experiences in the way this book aims to.

A brief account of Bill's life and the experiences that led him to our collaboration appears in the epilogue (page 161). Our stories are unsurprisingly different, but they reveal unexpected parallels that have resulted in our arriving at similar places as scholars. Perhaps what is of greatest relevance to this book is the improbability that both of us have achieved what our origins in no way portended. I urge you to read his story.

Introduction

Too often, the lives of people who climb out of dire circumstances and subsequently leave their mark on the world are portrayed as miracles of the human spirit or valorized as the main character of a rags-to-riches tale. Such narratives perpetuate the idea that only extraordinary individuals succeed against overwhelming odds; they focus on the individual qualities that led to a person's success while downplaying the *circumstances* that contributed to their success. Even less often is chance or luck assigned a major role in these success stories.

In 2018, scholars Alessandro Pluchino, Alessio Emanuele Biondo, and Andrea Rapisarda set out to investigate the "largely dominant meritocratic paradigm of highly competitive Western cultures [that] is rooted on the belief that success is due mainly, if not exclusively, to personal qualities such as talent, intelligence, skills, smartness, efforts, willfulness, hard work, or risk taking."[13] They conclude that, while talent contributes to a person's success, it's not the most talented people who are most successful; mediocre people who get lucky often surpass talented people.[14]

So, what's really going on? Evolutionary biologist Richard Lewontin suggests that forces outside human control play an essential role in the unfolding of human life; if we wish to understand living things, we must see that genes, organisms, and environments (Lewontin's

1

triple helix) are not separate entities.[15] Observers may attribute individuals' successes to their genes or to their environment—or the interactions of these factors. Lewontin argues that a critical element must be included if we are to understand how people's lives unfold: *chance.*[16] The American myth of rugged individualism (the belief that humans succeed against heavy odds solely through their individual talent, determination, and intelligence) obscures the role that the interaction of genes, environment, and chance play in shaping a person's path to success or failure.

In this introduction, we examine the roles that these three factors played in determining Yong's improbable path. We start with the role that chance events play in all aspects of our daily lives. We then describe some of the chance occurrences that helped shape Yong's life. Next, we consider how Yong's unfavorable environment offered him, paradoxically, opportunities to develop his interests and abilities. We also examine the role that Yong's personality traits may have played in his taking advantage of those opportunities. We conclude with an overview of the book.

Chance Encounters

Rags-to-riches and rugged individualism narratives ignore the fact that contingencies play a determinative role in individual success. Challenging these myths, Historian John Fea writes about the role contingency plays in events and people's lives:

> Contingency is . . . at odds with other potential ways of explaining human behavior in the past. Fatalism, determinism, and providentialism are philosophical or religious systems that teach that human behavior is controlled by forces—fate, the order of the universe, God—that are outside the control of humans . . . . [I]t is undeniable that we are all products of the macrolevel cultural or structural contexts that have shaped the world into which we have been born. Karl Marx suggested that human action

is always held in check by "the circumstances directly encountered, given, and transmitted from the past." It is unlikely that any proponent of contingency would deny that human behavior is shaped by larger cultural forces, but in the end, historians are in the business of explaining why people—as active human agents—have behaved in the past in the way that they did.[17]

Fea uses the example of the Union Army's victory at the Battle of Antietam during the U.S. Civil War that turned the conflict in favor of the Union (at the cost of 6,200 casualties).[18] Prior to the battle, a copy of General Robert E. Lee's battle plans fell into the hands of the Union command purely by chance. Fea quotes fellow historian James McPherson, who wrote that the "odds against the occurrence of such a chain of events must have been a million to one . . . yet they happened."[19]

Many of us are uncomfortable with the idea that chance occurrences have significantly shaped the world in which we live. We prefer to believe that there is a grand plan, that everything happens for a reason. The idea that success is not simply a function of our hard work and talent and that chance plays a significant role in how our lives unfold challenges both culturally embedded beliefs and our sense of control over our destinies. Echoing Duncan J. Watts, researchers Alessandro Pluchino, Alessio Emanuele Biondo, and Andrea Rapisarda write that:

People observe unusually successful outcomes and consider them as the necessary product of hard work and talent, while they mainly emerge from a complex and interwoven sequence of steps, each depending on precedent ones: if any of them had been different, an entire career or life trajectory would almost surely differ too.[20]

Let's examine some of the chance events that, had they turned out differently, would have changed the course of Yong's life. Of particular interest are random circumstances, events, or encounters that could have been debilitating, yet somehow moved Yong down the path to success.

> **Historical moment:** Yong was born between two events that killed millions of Chinese—the Great Leap Forward and the Great Cultural Revolution (page xvi). Social chaos, political uncertainty, internecine conflict, and continuing depravations characterized this period. As a boy born in an obscure village to the lowest class of peasants, Yong was in a vulnerable position. *If* he had been born earlier, he might have died of starvation, malnutrition, or disease. *If* he had been born later, he might not have had the opportunities that opened to him as a member of the lowest peasant class under the reforms of Chinese communist leader Deng Xiaoping (page 67).

> **Family:** Yong had the good fortune to be born into a family that placed no expectations on him, loved him, and allowed him to pursue his own path. Although illiterate, the family saw the value of schooling for Yong, especially as his poor health and weakness due to malnutrition made him ill-suited for manual labor. They supported him in whatever way they could as he worked his way up the educational system and allowed Yong to decide for himself how to live his life. *If* he had been born into another family, Yong might have faced familial expectations for what he should do and what he should become, which was common among his peers. He might also have been subjected to the physical and verbal abuse that undoubtedly left many children with physical and emotional scars.

> **Schooling:** Despite woeful conditions, Yong managed to succeed in school when no one else from his village did. He benefited from a few teachers who recognized his

potential and found ways to help him. He also benefited from Mao's educational reforms, which opened more opportunities for learning and brought experienced teachers to rural China (page 33). *If* he had not had the teachers that he had, gained access to Mao's reformed school system, and learned English instead of Russian (the required second language until the early 1960s), his path might have been very different.

> **Higher education:** Because his university career was delayed for a year due to his health issues, Yong qualified for a newly created English-teacher training program at the Sichuan Foreign Language Institute (SFLI), the flagship university for foreign language education and information in southwest China. The program covered student tuition and fees and offered access to a much wider world, including a bookstore that sold English-language books, journals, and magazines. Yong's success in computer and pedagogy courses earned him a spot on a research team, where he taught himself coding and statistics and wrote a program to analyze the survey data. *If* Yong had not been malnourished, he might have entered higher education the year before the English-teacher training program was created. *If* he had not been able to take and succeed in courses in computing and pedagogy, he might not have come to the attention of his professors or earned a spot on the research team.

This is, of course, a highly condensed account of a few of the chance events and contingencies Yong experienced in the first twenty-five years of his life. Each of us could chronicle our life in a similar way, identifying myriad random events, occurrences, encounters, and people that nudged us this way and that.

Along the way, chance events shape our environment to create unforeseen opportunities. Do we recognize opportunities? Do we take advantage of them? Let's examine some of the factors in Yong's environment that influenced his ability to capitalize on opportunities and embark on a path to success.

Environmental Factors

Yong's life illustrates how random events create unique and unforeseen paths. Changes in our environment present us with opportunities. Changes cause disequilibrium that people, if they are ready, can exploit. What factors in Yong's environment shaped him throughout his life?

> › **Yong's father's influence:** Yong's father was the most influential person in his early life. He was loving and caring toward Yong, allowed him the freedom to explore his interests and passions, and modeled an entrepreneurial approach to embracing opportunities rather than settling for the status quo.

> › **Village life:** Life in Yong's village was almost exclusively focused on survival. As members of the peasant class, villagers were fully occupied with feeding, clothing, and sheltering themselves just as their ancestors had done for thousands of years. Given this survivalist mentality, villagers did not judge how Yong spent his time, his chosen career path, or his adherence to social norms.

> › **Positive teacher relationships:** Yong had teachers who noticed his unique academic gifts and sought to encourage and mentor him, opening doors for him into higher education.

> › **Chinese education:** Historically, the Chinese have seen education as a means to a career (preferably as a

government official), prizing obedience to authority and rote memorization over all else. Student autonomy and critical thinking were typically punished, thus perpetuating a culture of student apathy, conformity, and acquiescence to authority. As a result, Yong's penchant for creative thinking, risk taking, innovation, and love of learning for its own sake made him an outlier who was unusually attuned to opportunities that others missed.

> **Global perspective:** As an adult, Yong traveled widely, developing friendships and collaborations with people from many different countries. As a result, he recognizes that no single culture or ethnicity can claim to be the bearers of "the truth" and that contributions to solving global problems can come from anyone.

Every person, even siblings in the same family, encounters a different set of environmental factors that shape who they are and offer various opportunities. This is an experience common to everyone. The difference is that some people recognize opportunities while others don't. Some people jump at the chance to walk through an open door while others hold back or turn away. Why was Yong able to recognize and take advantage of opportunities when many around him did not? Part of the answer to this may lie with his personality traits.

Influence of Personality

Research on the recognition of opportunities has focused almost entirely on entrepreneurial opportunities and the characteristics of those who seize promising ones. Most of the factors that researchers have identified and explored, such as social capital and prior knowledge of a given business sector, seem unhelpful in understanding Yong's ability to recognize opportunities.[21] However, one vein of research—focused on the psychological and cognitive factors that help explain the phenomenon—may help us understand

Yong's eye for opportunity. Researchers have found that personality traits play a vital role in a person's ability to recognize and capitalize on opportunities.[22, 23, 24]

Researchers Scott Shane, Nicos Nicolaou, Lynn Cherkas, and Tim Spector conclude, "Genetic factors account for a large part of the variance in opportunity recognition by influencing the probability that people will be open to experiences."[25] This research speaks to Lewontin's formulation and supports the idea that genes interact with both the environment and chance. Is it possible that certain personality traits could tip the scales, and increase the probability that some people are more likely than others to encounter promising opportunities?

Researcher Richard Wiseman became curious about this very question. Why do some people seem to be luckier than others?[26] Speculating that luck might not be totally random, he conducted several studies to learn more about what lucky people have in common and why they differ from those less lucky. When he studied the underlying dimensions of personality that psychologists had identified as universal, he found that luckier people shared three of the Big Five personality traits: extroversion, neuroticism, and openness.[27] How did these traits seem to play out in Yong's life?

> **Extroversion:** Evidence of Yong's extroversion includes his wide circle of friends across the globe and the numerous (over one hundred annually) invitations he receives to speak to business, educational, and governmental audiences. This speaks not only to the value others find in his ideas but also to his inherent likability and the genuine pleasure he takes in meeting and talking with others, especially those whose backgrounds differ from his own.

> **Neuroticism:** Wiseman notes that lucky people have "a relaxed attitude toward life."[28] The less anxious we are,

the less absorbed we are in worrying about what others think of us, the more attention we can focus on our environment, and, therefore, the more likely we are to see opportunities. Despite his full schedule, Yong seems relaxed whatever the situation. This is rooted, in part, in his wealth of experiences. Across his life, he has faced many adversities, and yet, he has not only survived but also thrived.

> **Openness:** Being open to new experiences or embracing a sense of adventure means that when opportunities do arise, lucky people tend to seize them. Research suggests that openness is moderately associated with intelligence and creativity.[29] Because Yong remains open to novel experiences, he embraces and thrives on an unconventional life of adventure and innovation.

The story of our lives is a complex fabric of many factors. As Lewontin observes, not only do our genes and environment intertwine, but chance also plays a major part in how that fabric is woven.[30] This is clear in Yong's life in the unique environmental factors that shaped his experiences, the chance encounters and events that presented unforeseen opportunities, and the inherent qualities and predispositions that allowed him to capitalize on them.

Book Overview

In this book, we strive to understand Yong's success by exploring the complex interplay of genes, environment, and chance. Each chapter examines a period of Yong's life through this lens, containing a brief vignette from that time, relevant historical factors, events that characterized that period of his life, and reflections on the implications for education.

In chapter 1, readers meet the boy from Sichuan Province: five-year-old Yong tagging along behind his father, the primary influence in his early life. Adults in Yong's rural village are concerned with feeding, clothing, and sheltering their families, which leaves Yong free of social expectations. As Yong uses his free time to devise entrepreneurial ventures around the village, he capitalizes on unlikely assets—his curiosity, rebellious nature, and penchant for rule-breaking—to follow his instincts toward what would become a scholarly life.

Chapter 2 describes how Yong teaches himself to read and enters school amid the upheaval of China's Cultural Revolution. Educational reforms after the establishment of the People's Republic of China (PRC) in 1949 allow Yong unprecedented access to school in rural China, as well as teachers who recognize his intellectual interests and gifts. Believing education to be primarily the means to a career, the Chinese have long valued diligent and compliant students. Relentlessly curious, questioning, and innovative, Yong is an outlier. This supports him as he masters the knowledge and skills needed to succeed in school and pass the extremely stringent university entrance exam—not once but twice. His facility with languages earns him entry into SFLI at a time when English-language teachers were in high demand.

Chapter 3 follows Yong during his time at SFLI, where he indulges his wide range of academic interests in the library and at a local bookstore. He also cultivates friendships with foreign faculty, opening opportunities to improve his English and learn more about the world beyond China. His academic success impresses his professors, who ask him to accompany a visiting scholar from Beijing. From the visiting scholar, Yong learns about the potential of desktop computers to run data analysis software. Asked to join an international team conducting research on English-language learners, Yong sees an opportunity to develop a program to analyze the survey data.

He teaches himself statistics and programming to create the first data analysis program for PCs in China.

In chapter 4, Yong joins a team of faculty who have been drafted to teach English in a remote city in Sichuan Province. Designated as the deputy team leader, Yong learns valuable leadership lessons and tests his group management abilities. One of his fellow volunteers, Xi, catches his eye, and they begin dating. During a visit back to SFLI, Yong's roommate convinces him to travel to the newly created special economic zone (SEZ) on Hainan Island. There, Yong and a partner create a successful translation business. Despite his success in Hainan, Yong finds himself missing the scholarly life and returns to SFLI to resume teaching and publishing.

Chapter 5 chronicles how communist leader Deng Xiaoping's economic reforms open China to Western culture and, in the late 1980s, spark debate on college campuses around the country. Eager to join the conversation, Yong opens his apartment as a salon where faculty and students gather and discuss the future of the country. As the tragic events of June 4, 1989, unfold in Tiananmen Square, the momentum Yong and others had felt building dies abruptly, leaving him despondent and aware that he needs to seek opportunities elsewhere. A visit from a U.S. professor to SFLI results in a friendship that, in turn, leads to an invitation to spend time at Linfield College, now Linfield University, in Oregon.

In chapter 6, Yong embarks on his first trip to the United States, an experience that expands his view of the world, education, and emerging technologies. During his time at Linfield, Yong teaches, makes friends, explores the emerging World Wide Web, and realizes that becoming a college professor will allow him to pursue the life he wants for himself and his family, which now includes a son, Yechen, in addition to his wife, Xi. Yong decides to pursue a graduate degree and gains admittance to the doctoral program at the University of Illinois Urbana-Champaign (UIUC). His prior work in developing statistical software lands him a teaching assistantship and a job in the computer lab and gains him credits toward his degree. He develops more software, including a platform to enable faculty to create their own websites and a program to organize message boards. Yong completes his master's degree in one year, welcomes his young family to the United States, and leaves an unsatisfactory job at Willamette University in Oregon for a more promising opportunity.

Chapter 7 begins with Yong and his family making a home at Hamilton College in New York, where Yong is part of a collaborative project between Hamilton College and Colgate University that enables students to take courses offered by both institutions. His successes earn him a tenure-track position at Michigan State University (MSU) in East Lansing, Michigan, where he works on a project to increase student engagement via online learning. He also creates an online submission platform for the American Educational Research Association (AERA) annual meeting. Success in these projects as well as his outstanding publications record and award-winning teaching earn him the title of University Distinguished Professor.

In chapter 8, we attempt to explain the central ideas and themes that run through Yong's prolific scholarly output. Over his career, he has engaged several of the seminal questions in education, such as, What kind of educational model best serves students? What are the consequences of schooling as a mechanism of state control? What are the pernicious effects of high-stakes assessment? How does personalized education benefit students? How can technology best serve education? How can promoting global thinking help us solve the world's most pressing problems?

The epilogue provides a brief overview of Bill's life and how he came to collaborate with Yong on this book. He describes the events that have shaped a worldview that is remarkably similar to Yong's.

CHAPTER 1

The Boy From Sichuan Province

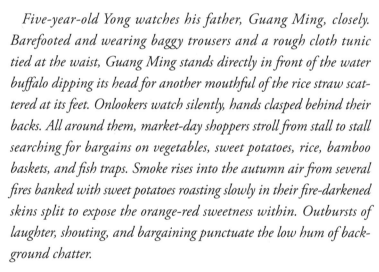

Five-year-old Yong watches his father, Guang Ming, closely. Barefooted and wearing baggy trousers and a rough cloth tunic tied at the waist, Guang Ming stands directly in front of the water buffalo dipping its head for another mouthful of the rice straw scattered at its feet. Onlookers watch silently, hands clasped behind their backs. All around them, market-day shoppers stroll from stall to stall searching for bargains on vegetables, sweet potatoes, rice, bamboo baskets, and fish traps. Smoke rises into the autumn air from several fires banked with sweet potatoes roasting slowly in their fire-darkened skins split to expose the orange-red sweetness within. Outbursts of laughter, shouting, and bargaining punctuate the low hum of background chatter.

Guang Ming steps forward, staring into the beast's eyes, and rests his hand on its snout. He smooths the buffalo's hide as he draws his hands down to its nose and pries open its mouth. He moves his hand slowly along the beast's molars, peers into its mouth, and sniffs its breath. When he finishes, he straightens up, withdraws his hand, and moves his attention to the animal's back, checking the joints in its ribs, spine, haunches, and legs. Stepping back, he surveys the beast again, nods to the man holding the bamboo rope that runs through the buffalo's snout, and makes a circling motion with his hand. The man whistles, barks an order, and leads the beast in a small, plodding circle. Yong's father watches the buffalo intently and then falls in behind the ponderous beast, observing its gait.

Once satisfied, Guang Ming approaches the man holding the rope, speaks a few quiet words, then slips his hand inside the sleeve of the man's tunic. The man reciprocates the gesture. Yong's father's hand moves beneath the rough cloth, then the rope-holder's hand moves in apparent response. Nodding slightly, Guang Ming withdraws his hand, turns, approaches a man in the crowd who has been watching the action, and repeats the sleeve ceremony.

Again, Yong notices his father nod ever so slightly. The onlooker unties a string attached to a small cloth bag from around his waist and hands it to Yong's father. He hands it to the man with the rope, who in turn hands the rope to Guang Ming. With a slight bow of his head, Guang Ming hands the rope to the buffalo's new owner. The watchers disperse, and Yong falls in behind his father, heading for one of the roasted sweet potato sellers.

———————————

In this chapter, we see that Yong's identity as a rule-bender, entrepreneur, and innovator begins with the example of his father, an unconventional man in rural China. Life in their remote and unremarkable village is about survival, which means residents are preoccupied with where their next meal will come from. No one has expectations for the diminutive boy wandering around the village in Guang Ming's wake. Inspired by his father's example, Yong tries out various money-making schemes, which typically fail. At the same time, he enjoys the freedom the lack of expectations affords him. This allows him to explore and discover both his strengths and weaknesses.

An Unconventional Father

Guang Ming was the earliest and most influential figure in Yong's life. Tagging along with his father, who took his firstborn son with him wherever he went, Yong observed and admired his father's varied interactions and activities around their village. Even at five years old, he appreciated the skill and knowledge involved in the buffalo-assessing practice he witnessed. He also noticed the respect that his father commanded from onlookers. Guang Ming knew a lot about many things in addition to buffalo assessment: animal husbandry, farming, fishing, bamboo weaving, business, and leadership. And he never seemed content to settle for the cards that life had dealt him—he was always looking for ways to improve his family's circumstances.

This drive had motivated Guang Ming. After his parents died and before Yong was born, Guang Ming negotiated good marriages for his two younger sisters, ensuring they would be respected and well-treated. This sense of responsibility spurred him to launch various ventures that would benefit not only his family but also his village. Yong watched his father secretly butcher pigs for other villagers, thereby helping them avoid having to share half of their animals with local government officials. He also learned that Guang Ming and a friend pushed a wooden handcart more than fifty miles to buy coal and sell it to villages during the return journey—an illegal private enterprise in Mao's China.[31] Although the government owned and operated all enterprises, this did not stop Yong's father and his friend from selling much-needed coal that was unavailable where they lived.

Yong's father understood the need to reach beyond the narrow self-interest of his family to help the collective. One of his larger ventures involved securing a contract from the village to raise fish in exchange for the use of one of the village ponds as a fish farm. At first, villagers supported the idea. When they saw how successful

Guang Ming's project was, the villagers opted not to renew the contract after the first year. They decided they could save the small fee they paid Yong's father and manage the fish farm themselves. It did not go well. Yong noted his father's response to the villagers' decision: persistently optimistic, he moved on and continued to look for ways to improve the lot of his family and the village. The experience of seeing his father challenge and even breech various norms and expectations, remain undeterred by setbacks, and continually scan his environment in search of ways to make life better for his family had a profound impact on Yong.

Yong's father is a central character in his story. Without consciously reflecting on his father's activities, he absorbed lessons that informed his own behavior and attitudes. Watching his father bend and sometimes break the rules for the sake of his family and community, Yong grew up with a healthy skepticism about all rules and regulations. Yong had no compunction about breeching restrictions that seemed to him impediments to where he wanted to go and what he wanted to do. He internalized the entrepreneurial and innovative spirit he saw in his father, who identified needs, envisioned ways to meet them, and enacted his plans to make his family's life better. He recognized the benefits of taking risks, being willing to try what others would regard as uncertain, even dangerous. Restless in mind and actions, he constantly probed prescribed limits for soft spots where he could push through. This was what Yong experienced as he grew up, a father unlike any other in his village.

The Unremarkable Village

Yong's home village of Xianggong Yuanzi, Yuechi County in Sichuan Province was, and remains, unremarkable. It boasted no historical sites, landmarks, or notable residents. There were no famous rivers or mountains nearby. It sat alongside other small villages in a narrow valley nestled between two hills. Rice fields were terraced into the hillsides, cascading down to the small creek that cut through the valley. Fields behind the village, which lacked sufficient water to support rice cultivation, grew sweet potatoes, vegetables, wheat, corn, peas, and sorghum. Bamboo grew everywhere in the village, and every family harvested the stalks to make sheets, baskets, and other containers.

When asked where he's from, Yong jokes that he comes from a village so poor that the inhabitants couldn't scratch together enough money to bribe government officials to put it on the list of poor villages eligible for special benefits. The funny thing is, it's not a joke. When Yong was born in 1965, roughly 80 percent of all rural Chinese lived in profound poverty. Because of collectivization and other policies during the Great Leap Forward, Sichuan Province was among the very poorest provinces as well as the most populated and rural of China's thirty provinces.

HISTORICAL CONTEXT

According to the World Bank, China's per capita annual income in 1965 was $98 in U.S. dollars.[32] That works out to about 27 cents a day. This average includes more prosperous urban areas such as Shanghai, Beijing, Nanjing, Guangzhou, Hangzhou, Tianjin, and so on. A conservative guess is that per capita income in rural areas such as Sichuan was far less, likely less than half the national average. At that time, China's per capita gross national product (GNP) was $1,070 USD; compare that to the United States, which was $7,890 USD. Rural communities were almost entirely subsistence economies. Though peasants relied on what they could grow, raise, forage, or harvest, they couldn't keep all the products of their labor—they were at the mercy of a government that prioritized urban areas, CCP officials, and the People's Liberation Army (PLA; China's armed forces). Villagers were often left without even the seeds needed for the following year's crop.

Yong was born a mere three years after the end of Mao's Great Leap Forward. This failed initiative, along with several natural disasters, was the primary cause of the Great Famine that claimed as many as forty-five million lives.[33] The famine hit remote rural communities particularly hard. Sichuan, Yong's home province, was the twenty-first most severely affected of the twenty-eight administrative units during the Great Famine.[34] Peasants such as those in Sichuan had been reduced to eating soil and boiled tree bark. Though the Great Leap Forward was over when Yong was born, peasants were still recovering, both physically and psychologically, from the trauma of the famine years. Childhood malnutrition was rampant, and starvation still occurred. As the prized firstborn male, Yong was as well-cared for as his family's circumstances allowed. Still, the lack of adequate nutrition in his childhood contributed significantly to his unusually small stature.

Like almost all rural Chinese villages at the time, Yong's community lacked electricity, sanitation or water systems, telecommunications, and paved roads—all the systems and conveniences that the West took for granted by the 1960s. Villagers used kerosene lamps for light. They relied on grass, straw, and—on rare occasions—coal for cooking. They fetched water from the village well each day. And they collected human and animal waste to fertilize the fields and gardens.

Although some of the other villages in the valley were less than half of a mile away, for Yong, they might as well have been in Switzerland. He regarded residents of other villages as foreign, untrustworthy, and even threatening. Only rarely did residents of different villages interact—the exception being when these foreigners were allowed to visit to draw water from the well in Yong's village during a severe drought. Only later, when he attended schools outside his village, did his suspicion of anyone not a resident of his village begin to ebb.

As Yong was growing up, the villagers he knew passively accepted their circumstances with the same silent resignation as that of their ancestors. Like peasants elsewhere, they viewed life as a never-ending cycle of seasons interrupted only by catastrophes such as floods, famines, and earthquakes. This view is reflected in the Chinese calendar, which represents a cycle of sixty years.[35] They also took in stride man-made disasters such as collectivization and the Great Leap Forward. The idea of defying or revolting against the government didn't occur to them. When orders came from officials, they did as they were told. They obediently brought their crops to town and handed them over when the government told them to do so, receiving in return paltry compensation at best. If they raised pigs and were told to deliver half of them to government officials for slaughter, they did so. Decades and centuries of unquestioning compliance to authority seemed ingrained in their psyches.

Yong's village had changed very little over the centuries. There had been no significant innovations or changes of any kind. The crops, farming methods, social customs, and rhythms of daily life— all were as they had been for centuries. The only people to leave the village were women who married into families from other villages. Villagers actively opposed attempts to bring about changes other than those initiated by the authorities, as Yong witnessed with his father's fish-farming scheme.

Despite the extreme poverty of his surroundings, Yong never thought of himself or his family as poor. Everyone in his village was equally poor. Poverty was the water they swam in, the air they breathed. As most humans do, he accepted his situation as the norm until experiences shifted his perspective. The lack of contact with anything beyond his immediate vicinity meant that, growing up, Yong had no other reality with which to compare his own.

Like most children, Yong played, did chores, spent time with his family and neighbors, and found pleasure in these simple experiences. He and his playmates remained largely unaware of the Cultural Revolution raging across the country. Neither he nor his sisters viewed their sparse meals of sweet potatoes, rice, and vegetables as meager. This was all they knew. In the lean months before the beans, sweet potatoes, and vegetables were ready for harvest and when few villagers had enough to eat, Yong's family borrowed wheat, corn, and rice (when available) from his uncles and aunts, who lived in relatively better places.

At times, when the only alternative was starvation, villagers harvested food crops before they were ready. This meant they merely postponed hunger and ate food that had not achieved its full nutritional value. Mothers sent children outside the village to forage for edible wild plants. During his childhood, Yong witnessed at least two people in his village starve to death. To save the village, the government sent silkworm cocoons to feed the dying people as well as seeds engineered to produce food within a month of planting, though this came at the cost of nutritional value.

Despite the hardships of these dire circumstances, Yong benefited from the lack of moral and social approbation—luxuries that those continually on the edge of starvation cannot afford. As a result, he avoided judgments and expectations from his family and community. This freed him from the social strictures that many children internalize, which constrain their actions and behaviors. It also meant he wasn't handed the preoccupation with amassing social capital, known as *guanxi*, that many of his urban peers inherited. Though this may seem like a disadvantage, it ultimately worked in Yong's favor. Free to follow his own interests, Yong spent much of his time launching entrepreneurial ventures around the village.

The Emerging Entrepreneur

Following his father's example, Yong initiated his own entrepreneurial ventures. One of his memorable efforts involved selling sweet water—water from the village well sweetened with a few pinches of purloined artificial sweetener—with a friend. Even decades later, Yong remembers the experience in vivid detail.

The boys labored up the dusty road, the bucket of water they carried growing heavier with each barefoot step. Below them, the village was coming alive. Loud voices filled the morning air and curses rang out as women discovered that someone had stolen their beans or sweet potatoes during the night. The crowing of roosters, the bellowing of water buffalo, the barking of dogs, the shrieking of children, the quacking of ducks—a cacophony of familiar sounds.

As they reached the midpoint of the road, they looked back and saw the first traveler of the morning—head down, walking stick in hand, bamboo basket on her back filled with sticks—plodding up the path. When she neared, Yong called out, "Sweet water, Auntie! Only two pennies!"

His taller companion looked down at Yong. "She can't hear you. Your voice is too weak."

Then, he bellowed out, "Your mouth must be dry, Auntie. Our sweet water is just two pennies."

As the walker approached, she glanced at the boys and continued on her way. And so it went all morning. A few dozen villagers climbed the hill. Despite the heat and their exertion, none took the boys up on their offer.

By afternoon, the boys had drunk most of the sweet water to slake their thirst, and hunger overwhelmed their fading hopes for success. Dejected, they carried their empty bucket back to Yong's house.

Like many successful entrepreneurs, Yong was undeterred by this early failure. He went on to launch other enterprises. For instance, he launched a rabbit-raising start-up. Unfortunately, the rabbits lived up to their reputation and reproduced so rapidly that the flourishing family tunneled under the dirt floor of Yong's house, alarming his father. So, rather than providing income, the rabbits provided several tasty stews for the family.

As a five-year-old, Yong ventured again into the culinary business, this time in the sweet potato trade. Given that sweet potatoes are a staple throughout rural China, Yong thought of them as a likely commodity for commercialization. At that time, sweet potatoes were a staple of villagers' diets because they were well-suited to the climate, thrived in the loamy soil that lacked the water needed for rice cultivation, and lasted for weeks (sometimes months) if stored in a cool, dark root cellar. Not only are sweet potatoes full of beta-carotene, but they also contain vitamins B6 and C and are a good source of fiber, iron, and potassium. They boost the immune system, reduce inflammation, and help maintain healthy eyesight. In addition, their high caloric content makes them especially valuable at times when food is scarce.[36]

Having convinced his father to stake him to a few sweet potatoes, Yong hoisted a bamboo backpack containing the spuds and walked to the town market a few miles away. He quickly discovered he was ill-suited to sweet-potato marketing, though. As the morning progressed, he moved farther and farther from his potatoes. While his competitors lustily cried out to passing customers, vouching for the quality of their tubers, Yong was undone by his shyness. As a small child trying to compete with aggressive adults, he was understandably timid.

Unlikely Assets

Though Yong's quiet nature scuttled his sweet potato venture, it did nothing to dampen his insatiable curiosity. One constant source of fascination for Yong throughout childhood was the village loudspeaker, which was installed and controlled by the government. Three times each day for an hour, disembodied voices spoke in odd accents about happenings in a wider world. The loudspeaker was a village's only connection to events beyond their immediate horizon.[37]

Yong heard about Communist Party meetings taking place in Beijing, memorials for national leaders and war heroes, readings from Mao's works, revolutionary songs and music, and stories of self-sacrificing workers or soldiers who had died for the Cultural Revolution and the Party. He also learned about the threat that capitalist nations such as the United States posed and the need for China to prepare for war. The voices spoke of places, people, and events completely foreign to him, and this ever-present invisible narrator spurred his imagination and curiosity as he tried to decipher what he heard. The constant stream of information hinted at a world much more eventful and exciting than his. From early in his life, Yong was eager to learn more about this mysterious world.

Not only did Yong enjoy the loudspeaker's stories, but he also wondered how the thing worked. He wanted to know more about the technology. He imagined that it had to be a system of hollow bamboo through which the voices traveled. Examining a loudspeaker wire downed in a storm forced him to revise his theory. Not only did he learn that the wire wasn't hollow, but he also discovered, painfully, the wire was electrified.

Another mystery Yong felt compelled to unlock came in the form of a rare childhood toy. Like rural children elsewhere, Yong and the other village children were accustomed to fashioning toys from whatever was at hand. They made playthings from sorghum straw, paper, and seeds from the tung tree. They played games with discarded cigarette packs and matchstick boxes.

Given the everyday objects Yong was used to playing with, he became mesmerized by the first manufactured toy he received from a relative. One year, Yong and his family walked the two and a half hours to visit one of his maternal uncles to celebrate Spring Festival. Spring Festival in China is the equivalent of Christmas, New Year, and Thanksgiving all rolled into one holiday. Regardless of how long or arduous the journey, nearly all Chinese return to their home communities to spend time with family and friends, eat together, and exchange gifts. To Yong's surprise, his uncle gave him a small ball, the first manufactured toy he had ever held. Once he returned home, Yong shared his ball with the other village children, who were impressed with the rare toy. They took turns all afternoon bouncing and catching it, passed it around among themselves, and invented their own games. Only when it became too dark to see did they stop playing. Yong took his ball home, pleased that he had earned new regard as proprietor of a novel plaything.

Although curiosity can lead to gratifying discoveries, it can also produce unintended consequences. Curious to know why the ball bounced, Yong considered various explanations as he lay in bed that night. Maybe, he thought, there was a small animal or something else inside that caused the ball to bounce. He kept thinking about it for several days. Unable to contain his curiosity, he finally decided on a course of action: he would cut the ball open. This proved to be more difficult than he imagined. He had no tools to speak of. The family did have a pair of scissors, but they weren't up to the task. Finally, he used the family's all-purpose cleaver. When he succeeded . . . he found nothing inside. Deeply disappointed, Yong tried in vain to stitch the ball back together. In this case, Yong paid a high price for his curiosity.

Another trait that sometimes got the better of him was his penchant for rule-breaking. Yong often watched other children playing in the village pond, resenting his father's command to avoid the water. This made a deep impression on Yong because his father had no other rules. Because he regarded this rule as not entirely rational, Yong decided to disregard it; he was determined to learn to swim.

On a hot summer day, as he watched his peers enjoying themselves, he followed other boys into the pond. When he was over his head, panicking, he began to move his arms and legs as he had seen other boys do. Eventually, Yong found that he could keep his head above water. When he surfaced, he was startled to hear his father yelling and see him gesticulating angrily from the bank. Guang Ming was a man of calm demeanor; it was rare to see him so worked up. When the yelling didn't work, Yong's father resorted to throwing small stones in the water near his son, an attempt to force him to the shore. Frightened by his father's unprecedented behavior, Yong dodged the stones and stayed in the water. After a while, his father gave up and stomped away, exasperated.

When Yong was sure his father had left, he climbed out of the pond. Too scared to go home, he hid in a rice field until one of his sisters came calling for him and persuaded him to come home and face the music. This was the only time Yong remembers his father spanking him. The spanking was perfunctory because, by chance, one of his uncles was visiting. In the end, Yong decided the crime was worth the punishment. As an adult, Yong came to understand that his father was reacting from fear of the water—unable to swim, Guang Ming worried the water would rob him of his firstborn son.

Though Yong's curiosity and rebellious nature led him into occasional trouble in his youth, they also served as assets. The absence of rules freed Yong to explore, learn from experience, and test out his ideas. Later in life, Yong would cite this absence of rules and restrictions as enabling him to trust his instincts and disregard rules when they got in the way of his plans—factors that contributed to his success.

Reflections

Given the details of Yong's earliest environment, few people would predict he would become an internationally recognized scholar. What factors in his early life set the boy from Sichuan Province on the path to becoming a global citizen?

Reflecting on his childhood, Yong feels that what most people regard as disadvantages he was able to harness as assets. He doesn't see his story as a conventional tale of a heroic individual drawing on reserves of grit and determination to overcome great odds. Rather, he sees his circumstances, weaknesses, and constraints as being advantageous. His village may have been remote and poor, but that also meant he faced no expectations or social pressures, allowing him to pursue his own interests. His father, Guang Ming, may have been an illiterate peasant, but his fellow villagers' resignation to the bleak status quo opened up opportunities for him to devise entrepreneurial ventures. Watching his father find opportunities that others overlooked encouraged Yong to do the same: to exploit rather than submissively accept his circumstances. He may have had few toys and limited information about the outside world, but this allowed his curiosity and imagination to flourish. His family was unable to provide him with activities that urban children enjoyed, leaving Yong free to wander, explore, and daydream as he pleased.

Our intent is not to glorify poverty. Poverty has multiple devastating effects on children.[38] Persistent poverty can dramatically reduce opportunities for social and economic mobility as well as cause debilitating, chronic health problems.[39] All societies benefit from efforts to reduce poverty and to provide extra support for children of low-income families. Governments should institute policies to reduce poverty, improve health, and increase access to powerful knowledge and skills for children from low-income homes. Even in straitened circumstances, parents and educators can find ways to support these children in the classroom. By adopting asset thinking and committing to heart-centered learning, teachers can create a dynamic environment for all students to maximize their potential.

In *Equitable Instruction, Empowered Students*, educator Carissa McCray contrasts deficit thinking that focuses on what student lack with an asset model in which educators identify and seek to build on the assets students possess:

> Deficit thinking shows up in the way teachers focus on what students do not have, what they cannot do, and how far behind they are rather than drawing on what students *do have* that can drive success. Equitable teaching disrupts a deficit model and embraces an asset model.[40]

Asset-based education is not to be confused with high expectations. The absence of high expectations for a child's future may, on first consideration, appear to be a handicap. Shouldn't parents be encouraging their children to "reach for the stars"? This may work for some children. In other cases, however, parental expectations can be a burden.[41] However, this is not the primary narrative that parents or teachers typically hear. Evidence suggests that students' aspirations for their future—one of the assets they bring with them—are more closely associated with their actual achievement than parents' expectations.[42] More accurately, each student appears to have a sweet spot where their aspirations and expectations from parents and teachers converge in a supportive context.[43]

Educational rhetoric and policies in the United States and across the globe encourage parents and educators to hold high expectations for students as a way to boost achievement.[44] The belief is that holding high expectations for children from low-income communities will help them improve academic performance. This belief has found its way into a range of policy vehicles including curriculum standards, standardized testing, and grade retention. Holding high expectations alone is not enough; it must be paired with a caring environment if students are to reap the benefits.[45]

In addition to holding high expectations for students, parents and teachers must build strong, healthy relationships with them to promote a sense of belonging in the classroom. In *Mindful School*

Communities, Christine Mason, Michele Rivers Murphy, and Yvette Jackson note that:

> Humanistic psychologist Carl Rogers believed that in order for individuals to grow, they need an environment that provides positive relationships and interactions with healthy personalities, along with genuineness (openness and self-disclosure), acceptance (being viewed with unconditional positive regard or love), and empathy (being listened to and understood).[46]

Yong's story illustrates the benefits of belonging and connectedness. His family loved and supported him within their extremely limited means. They accepted uncritically that he was unlikely to succeed as a farmer like his father and the other men in the village. They trusted that Yong could find his own path. Moreover, unlike families in wealthier urban areas, Yong's family felt no social pressure to ensure their children excelled academically and pursued a high-status profession. Without external expectations for who he should be or what he should do or become, Yong was free to explore and imagine. Unburdened by expectations, he experienced his family's unconditional love and support, enabling him to explore, cultivate, and express his own nature.

CHAPTER 2

The Budding Scholar

Seven-year-old Yong sits alone at a stone desk in the village class-room. The walls splotched with mildew display various Chinese characters painted in red. Voices float into the room from outside, where classmates play on the dusty school grounds. Yong has no desire to join them. Before him is a book, Collected Writings of Chairman Mao. *A box of identical books with their bright-red covers has just arrived, and Yong is excited to find out what they contain.*

Yong has memorized the few Chinese characters his teacher writes on the chalkboard each day. He also notices characters painted on banners and walls as he walks through his village and nearby town. The walls of his house include weatherworn tombstones that his father scrounged from nearby fields, some with indecipherable script. Yong likes to trace the characters on the stones with his finger, trying to make sense of them. Characters, he feels, represent the unknown. He senses that deciphering them will open a world beyond his vil-lage, a world he envisions from the stories told through his village's loudspeaker. Yong longs to know more about this world.

He opens the book and searches the first page for familiar charac-ters. Most of them he doesn't understand. But a few he does. He finds the simple character that means work. *Then the character for* team. *Next, the character for* big. *As he identifies more and more characters on the page, Yong experiences a thrill as the meaning of the text begins to form in his mind.*

The world in which he lives begins to transform from a world of familiar objects to a world of texts. Hungry to learn, he searches everywhere for reading material of any kind. For a time, his father works at a noodle shop in the village, which Yong visits after school. When they dry, his father wraps the noodles in paper, often book pages and bits of old newspapers. Yong picks these up and reads them before they go to the customers. They are merely article or story fragments, but Yong takes this as a challenge to fill in the blanks with his imagination. Yong uses the context provided by familiar words to guess at the meaning of new words. In this way, he soon teaches himself to read fluently at a time when most of his classmates are still struggling or have given up. He is the first in his family and among the first in his village to master reading.

＋————————————＋

In this chapter, we examine how Chinese educational and political reforms in the 1960s facilitate Yong's access to school. Thanks to his determination, passion for reading, and supportive teachers, Yong's natural love of learning leads to early academic success and puts him on the scholar's path. His hunger for knowledge makes him an outlier in traditional Chinese educational culture in which schooling is a means to an end, not an end in itself. Despite his tendency to ignore some rules in high school and his relative indifference to mathematics and science, he passes the stringent university entrance exam (the infamous *gaokao*) not once but twice. He is then selected to begin an English-teacher preparation program at SFLI in Chongqing, Sichuan Province.

Education Reform

Yong's passion for knowledge and the doors to the wider world it opened didn't align with the traditional Chinese view of education. Despite its reverence for learning and knowledge, China has a long history of viewing education as a utilitarian endeavor.[47] The Sui Dynasty (581–618 AD) saw education as a means to identify people who were diligent, knowledgeable about rituals and traditions, committed to the ruling dynasty, and capable of memorizing volumes of information. In service of this goal, the emperor instituted the imperial examination (*keju*), which included questions about the Confucian classics, military strategy, civil law, revenue and taxation, agriculture, and geography. The *keju* was designed to identify men who would become competent and compliant bureaucrats and who could be counted on to effectively apply the laws, diligently perform their duties, loyally serve the emperor, and uncritically uphold the existing order. The system ensured that the emperor maintained control over the affairs of state and the mechanisms of governance as well as forestalled any challenges to his authority.

Aspirants studied and mastered the Confucian syllabus that emphasized obedience to those in authority and reverence for inherited knowledge. Successful candidates demonstrated the highest regard, loyalty, and deference to whomever was above them in the state hierarchy and, ultimately, to the emperor. Roughly 5 percent of those who attempted the *keju* passed. Despite the odds, the years of preparation were worth it. Government officials commanded not just respect and deference but a comfortable life for their families and advantages for their children. Because the incentives were so great, anyone who might have the potential for independent thought forfeited this potential in exchange for status, wealth, and reverence for codified knowledge. This view of education continued to be the status quo for centuries.

HISTORICAL CONTEXT

Despite the Sino-Soviet split in 1960, when all Soviet specialists left China,[48] the educational system they helped create remained in place. Heavily influenced by their former advisors, Chinese officials adopted a Soviet educational model designed to identify and promote a technical elite capable of running the country. The model featured state-controlled curricula and didactic teaching, both of which complemented Chinese educational traditions and societal norms.[49] Policies and systems that promoted and maintained the power of the few at the expense of the masses became a primary target of Mao and his supporters during the Cultural Revolution. In fact, the education system became target number one for reformers. The goal was to create a much more egalitarian system based on Mao's ideas and philosophy. As an educator at the time asserted, "Our school system has been a mishmash of Confucianism, Deweyism, and Sovietism. We are going to change all this by making our schools really Chinese and really socialist by using the thought of Mao Tse-tung."[50]

Yong was fortunate to enter school in 1972 during a time when Mao was reforming rural education. Despite the excesses and violence of the Cultural Revolution, many of the changes it brought to rural areas were positive and historic. The Central Committee issued a directive in 1966 stating: "The task of the Cultural Revolution is to reform the old educational system and educational philosophy and methodology."[51] As a result, local governments built primary schools in many villages that, prior to the late 1960s, had never had schools. The central government also suspended the exams required for promotion to the next level of schooling.[52] American scholar and author Suzanne Pepper summarized the goal of the educational reforms in this way: "The single, unified nationwide objective was to produce laborers with socialist consciousness and culture."[53] The push for education resulted in primary school enrollment in some rural areas approaching 100 percent by 1976.

Yong benefited from another general policy during the Cultural Revolution that returned many urban teachers to their villages. As a result, teachers with at least a middle school education were available to staff some of the new schools. Although, in some cases, teachers were selected based not on their education but on their political status, even illiterate villagers understood the value of teachers with at least a middle school education. In one case, when villagers discovered that a teacher from a Shanghai college had been sent to their community as an assistant pig farmer, they successfully persuaded the village school committee to make him their children's teacher. This speaks to the power over their schools that local communities exercised during the Cultural Revolution's educational reforms.[54]

Academic Success

Most satisfying for Yong was realizing that he had found his *métier*, something that few others in his world could claim. His slight stature and subpar athletic skills had consigned him to the ignominy of being the last pick for any physical activity. When a young woman arrived in the village to recruit students for the village school, his father (as a village leader) invited her into their house. Yong sat beside his father as the woman explained how to register for admittance. When Yong's father asked if he was interested, he did not hesitate. Though Yong was only six, technically too young to start school, he impressed the teacher so much that she waived the age requirement.

His interests and talent aligned well with the changes occurring in Chinese education at that time. The reforms that Mao's government instituted stripped the Confucian artifacts from the curriculum.[55] In keeping with his views of education, the emphasis shifted from the purely academic to the practical. Under Mao's direction, educational officials truncated and revamped the curriculum. The study of modern texts largely replaced memorization and recitation of ancient texts. Although Mao wrote to serve his own interests and further the reform wing of the Communist Party, he was an accomplished poet who had also written a history of modern China from 1840. Western scholar David Milton describes his writings as "congenial to the Chinese mind and experience."[56]

Yong's school texts included inspiring stories and poems of heroes of the Revolution. He found the stories of children who had bravely sacrificed their lives in defense of socialism and their commune inspiring. He learned about peasants and soldiers who fought selflessly against counterrevolutionaries and reactionaries intent on restoring pre-Revolution capitalism and cronyism. Though the intent of the textbooks was less educational than political, more propaganda for the Cultural Revolution than literature, Yong was unaware of the political subtext and simply enjoyed the narratives. Even more, he enjoyed the pleasure of making sense of the text, regardless of any underlying message.

The educational reforms also addressed teacher behavior and teacher-student relationships. Teachers were encouraged to cultivate authentic relationships with their students in place of the rigidity and formality typical of Soviet and classical Chinese educators. As people who relied on their minds rather than their backs to work, teachers were held in low esteem. Teaching was commonly viewed as an entry-level job.[57] Although teachers had traditionally commanded high respect, their status declined precipitously after 1949. Despite this, Yong was fortunate to have a few teachers with the perspicacity to recognize his potential and support his development despite the official preference for students who were good laborers and Party loyalists.

In second grade, Yong's teacher made him a teaching assistant, commonly called a "class monitor."[58] As the sole teacher for forty or fifty students, she was also the principal and taught all subjects for the mixed-grade class of first and second graders. Unlike Yong, most of the students were bored and, as a result, passed the time harassing their classmates, chatting, and even fighting with one another. The teacher taught groups of students in ten-minute segments. The class monitors taught the other students, helped those who were having difficulties, and attempted to maintain discipline. They also assisted with group tasks such as collecting the bundles of fresh grass that students were required to bring with them.

Yong's success enabled him to continue beyond the first two years of elementary school to grades 3–5 in another school in a different village where his teacher had more training. Again, the reforms benefited Yong's interests and talents. Prior to 1966, the Chinese school system resembled those in Western countries: a funnel that grew increasingly narrow to produce an educated elite. Mao installed a radically different model intended to increase literacy and reward students based less on academic achievement and more on contributions to their communities and commitment to the Revolution and the Party.

The reformed system was a five-two-two model (five years of primary school, two years of middle school, and two years of high school), and government officials eliminated the exams previously required to advance up the system.[59] In addition to village primary schools, the government established middle schools (grades 6 and 7) and high schools (grades 8 and 9) in nearby towns. Reducing the length of pre-college education served financial as well as political goals. Funding that previously went to grades 10–12 could be reallocated to elementary and middle schools, benefiting more of Mao's supporters, rural farmers, and factory workers and further solidifying support for the Party, Mao, and Revolutionary principles.[60]

The middle school that Yong and others from his and nearby villages attended was about two miles away in the town. Although the road was often muddy and cold on his bare feet in winter and sear-ingly hot in summer, Yong passed the time talking with other stu-dents or simply daydreaming. Although he had visited the grounds of the middle school a few times before, he found the size of the school overwhelming. His visits had been occasioned by memorials, in 1976, for three giants of the Revolution: Zhou Enlai in January, Zhu De in July, and Mao Zedong in September.

Students from all the surrounding villages gathered on what was to Yong an immense playground. The number of students and school officials assembled on the stone stage at the front amazed Yong, as did the orderliness of the ceremonies. Hundreds of children stood silently in ruler-straight rows listening (or pretending to listen) to the interminable tributes to the fallen heroes whose faces loomed on banners over the stage.

When Yong returned to the middle school as a student in 1977, he was still in awe of the size of the school with its multiple class-rooms and what, to him, were legions of teachers and students. Life at home changed as well. As Yong succeeded and moved up the grade levels, his family and neighbors grew to respect him even more. Despite the Maoist antipathy to Confucius and the values and education he propagated, the Confucian respect for scholars and knowledge is deeply ingrained in the Chinese psyche and permeates all levels of society.

From this point of view, learning is valued and understood almost entirely as a means to material success and social standing. That learning could be an end in itself, that discovery can be a source of satisfaction and enjoyment and need not be justified by its use was, and continues to be, an unorthodox concept throughout Chinese history, society, and culture. Although explicitly rejecting Confucianism and a privileged bureaucracy, the Maoist educational philosophy doubled down on the view that only knowledge that had immediate, practical application was valuable. Remarkably, despite these circumstances, Yong was able to cultivate his curiosity and his desire to discover and unlock the mysteries of written languages.

Outsider Status

Resigned to his inadequacies in virtually all things physical, Yong increasingly realized that he could succeed at school and pass the required exams when few of his peers could. In fact, most students viewed school as serving practical ends and dropped out before the end of primary school. What, they wondered, was the point of school if their future was as farmers?[61] In addition to vilifying the idea of learning for learning's sake, the Cultural Revolution had annihilated the idea of education as a means of improving people's social standing. True social mobility no longer existed in Maoist China. Long viewed as a means of improving social status, schools and learning were now fully enlisted in the cause of enculturating Chinese youth with Revolutionary values, beliefs, and spirit. Professor Martin Singer writes that Mao's goal was to "proletarianize educational opportunity."[62]

Yong's success in school and his lack of success in the physical and social realms gradually relieved him of expectations that he would, like most his peers, perform family and community chores or join others for games and play. He understood that, given his diminutive size and limited physical capabilities, he would never achieve much in the activities and work that the Maoist educational reforms valorized. This reinforced his belief that his future lay not in the fields but in the classroom. His success, the pleasure he took in intellectual discovery, and his growing confidence in his scholarly abilities gave him a quiet confidence, a belief in the path he had chosen as well as a sense of himself as an outsider, separate from his peers, his village, and even his family. The lack of expectations served him well. School was a world in which he felt comfortable, and not only succeeded where others did not but also exercised a level of control unlike any he experienced elsewhere.

Yong's understanding of himself as an outsider in school mirrored his growing awareness of himself as an outsider to his family. Although they supported him to the extent their meager circumstances allowed, his uneducated parents and siblings did not share his interests in school and academic learning. They did not understand his fascination with school and books, yet they supported him, trusting his instinct for his own path. From the time he entered middle school, his father deemed him to be a *dushuren*, or "book-reading person." As a result, he was no longer expected to carry out the chores required of other boys in the village, such as taking water buffalo to graze, gathering wild grasses to feed the pigs, harvesting sweet potatoes, working the rice fields, and performing other manual tasks.

One day, as he read a torn page salvaged from the noodle shop, his father came into the room and sat down beside him. The walls of the house were decorated with certificates of merit for Yong's school achievements and good behavior. His father explained that he believed Yong was the incarnation of a *wenquxing*—an ancient Taoist deity believed to be the patron saint of literary scholars and exam-takers. Therefore, his father continued, he felt he could offer Yong no advice on his education. Yong understood that his father recognized that his role was to support him in whatever way he could on the path Yong had chosen for himself. While other children bore the weight of their family's expectations for their future, Yong benefited from his family's *laissez-faire* attitude and respect for his decisions. In his second year in middle school, when Yong's teacher allowed him and a few other boys to stay at the school overnight to afford them more time to prepare for the high school entrance exam, Yong's father happily agreed.[63]

When Yong was fourteen in 1979, he was among the few to pass the exam to continue to high school. Under the five-two-two scheme, high school consisted of only two years of study. The high school served students from an even larger area than had the middle school.

As part of the 1966 educational reforms, rural communes across the provinces had built high schools. In some areas, enrollment and graduation rates were more than thirteen times higher than in the seventeen years prior to the Cultural Revolution.[64] Schools scrambled to find enough teachers with the result that many had scarcely more formal education than their charges. Working-class pedigree and devotion to the Revolution often trumped formal education as qualifications. Just like farmers, teachers were typically paid in work points that could be exchanged for grain, a system that shifted some of the cost of schooling to the local communes. This allowed direct funding for education without the fiscal burden of a tax bureaucracy.[65]

Because the high school was more than ten miles away from his village, Yong lived in the dormitory, which housed forty or more students in a large open room. With no bedding, Yong persuaded a friend from his area to allow him to sleep on his bed and share his quilt. His small size worked in his favor as he took up very little space. On cold winter nights, the warmth of his bedmate was a bonus.

The daily routine, beginning around 6:00 a.m., included a cold-water wash, traditional exercises, teeth brushing, a quick and meager breakfast, then classes. As the school didn't provide meals, the boys brought their own food that the school cook placed in a large steamer. Sweet potatoes and occasionally a little rice constituted Yong's daily breakfast. The forty-five-minute morning classes, punctuated by short breaks, included mathematics and Chinese language followed by English. Students then ate lunch—as the school had no cafeteria, students ate outside in fair weather and in the dormitory when it rained. Lunch was followed by a mandatory nap.

Afternoon classes included more mathematics, physics or chemistry, geography, and history. When classes ended around 4:30 p.m., the boys had free time. While most of the students played sports or games, Yong used the time to indulge in his favorite pastime—reading. A few of his classmates also preferred reading or doing schoolwork to the rough and tumble of the playground. These boys became Yong's posse. Evening studies typically started at 7:00 p.m. and ended around 9:30 p.m.

On Saturday afternoons after classes, Yong walked the ten miles back to his village. At home, he shared a meal with his family, typically sweet potatoes and rice with salt fried in lard. On Sunday afternoons, he made the return trip to his school, carrying on his back a bamboo basket with twenty pounds of sweet potatoes and a handful of rice to feed him for the week.

The twenty-mile round-trip walk was a trial for Yong, chronically malnourished (as were roughly half of all children in rural China) and small of stature. Nothing attests more definitively to his love of learning—and of his family—than his willingness to make this arduous weekly trek. Yong drew on a deep well of grit and his belief in the new horizons that knowledge was opening. The prospect of not eating for the week was also a powerful motivator.

When the weather turned hot, Yong and his classmates slept outside, as their almost window-less dormitory transformed into a sauna scented with the sweat of forty adolescent boys. Another advantage of sleeping outside was the chance to sneak away from the school under the cover of darkness, an opportunity too tempting for Yong to ignore.

Anti-Authoritarian

Taking advantage of the darkness one warm night, Yong and his posse stealthily scaled the fence surrounding the school and headed into the nearby town to a movie theater. Movies during the 1970s and early 1980s invariably glorified the heroes of China's ancient and recent past and often featured patriotic sacrifices of courageous peasants and the People's Liberation Army fighting the Japanese and the Kuomintang, the nationalist revolutionary party that had been supported by the Soviet Union.

The boys were exhausted by the time they returned to school after the movie. Their teacher, less than amused, was waiting for them. Yong was surprised by the lenient punishments that ensued: he and his classmates were made to copy long poems or essays late into the night. As the leader, Yong was assigned extra copying. All in all, the boys agreed the adventure was well worth the candle. Yong felt no shame for his part in the event. He reasoned that his actions had harmed no one and had, in fact, brought cheer into his life and the lives of his classmates. While a couple of the boys were embarrassed to be caught breaking the rules, Yong was not. No harm, no foul.

Another movie adventure illustrates Yong's ability to persuade others to follow his lead—sometimes into trouble. During the summer before he went to high school, Yong recruited a group of boys from his village to walk to the county city to watch a movie in the movie theater, an experience they'd never had before. After walking for more than three hours, they each paid five cents to watch the movie. After it ended, they had to walk for three hours to return home. Having watched films and read stories depicting the PLA's support of peasants, the boys decided to try to hitch a ride from a passing military vehicle. When they saw a PLA truck coming, an infrequent event, they lay down on the road, hoping the driver would stop and pick them up. Instead, the boys scrambled out of the way as the truck roared by, and the driver leaned out the window cursing at them. So much for the peasant-PLA alliance. Wearily, the disappointed boys resumed their dusty trudge back home.

Yong's disregard for authority reaches all the way back to middle school when he used a small stick to chip away at the stucco wall against which his desk sat. He eventually gouged out a hole that allowed him to peek outside. When confronted by his teacher, he felt no remorse or embarrassment. He knew that the hole could be easily patched. Yong's imperviousness to shame and to adult chastisements that made his classmates' cheeks burn freed him from a tool that those in authority have long wielded to manipulate children's emotions and behaviors. Underlying this obduracy was an introspective rationality and self-assurance grounded in the trust his family, especially his father, placed in him, as well as a belief in himself.

Without consciously identifying as a rebel, from early in his life, Yong was suspicious of and silently resistant to authorities. Although they never discussed the matter, Yong sensed that his father understood and accepted that his son's way of thinking diverged from the political orthodoxy of the times. His father was at peace with this.

Although independent-minded and self-confident, Yong was not completely impervious to peer pressure. On the day he was to start high school, Yong followed an older classmate from his village to a nearby field where a group of boys were playing cards. Never having gambled before, Yong couldn't truly understand what was going on. Shortly, he found himself fleeced of all his money, the eight yuan that his parents had scraped together to pay his school tuition for the semester. Totally distraught, Yong began to cry. His friend took pity on him and demanded that the other boys return the money. The lessons Yong learned from this experience he carried through high school and beyond: don't gamble, and befriend at least one ally who always has your back.

As the forays to the movies with other boys show, at least a few of his classmates found Yong likeable. His humor and cleverness were appealing, especially to other academically minded boys. At the same time, he wasn't popular, which didn't bother him in the least. As Xiaorong Shao, a contemporary of Yong's, has written, "A popular child back then was from a poor family class, anti-intellectual and obeying the central government regardless of his or her academic performance."[66] Although he belonged to the poorest peasant class, Yong didn't fit the other two criteria for popularity.

From the time he could read, Yong's path was that of an intellectual. Ideas and information were for him playthings and sources of pleasure. He found learning not merely satisfying but exciting. As for obeying the government, he was suspicious of and resistant to authority without explicitly identifying himself as a rebel.

The Formidable Gaokao

At the end of his second year in high school, Yong, like hundreds of thousands of students all over China, sat for the recently reinstated *gaokao*, the annual standardized college entrance exam. The exam had two tracks: one in science and mathematics and the other in humanities and literature. A third track, in foreign languages, was discontinued a year later. Yong was among the 4 percent of exam-takers who passed the *gaokao* in 1981, which made him eligible to enter a university. Humanities and literature, the subjects that most interested Yong and in which he performed best, were academically *déclassé*, judged the last refuge of weak students.[67] This pejorative opinion in no way diminished his love of these subjects.

Yong's experience contrasted with that of students in relatively more prosperous parts of the country and whose families were wealthier and better connected thanks to their social connections, or *guanxi*. Professor Xiaorong Shao's upbringing, described in *The Broken Cart: A Rural Girl's Journey Through China's Cultural Revolution and Beyond*, presents a useful case for comparison. Shao was born in Northwest China in Shaanxi Province in 1962. Her family's village was forty miles from Xi'an, the capital of the province where her father worked as a water engineer. Her father came from a relatively prosperous family and her mother from a poor one— though both of her parents came from peasant stock. Shao's family was designated as landlord class during the Cultural Revolution, despite the small size of the family's land parcel. Her father's status as a Communist Party member and revolutionary cadre did not mitigate their scorned landlord class status. The family relinquished their house to a poor peasant-class family and was given a cave house in which to live. Shortly afterward, however, when the village political working group discovered that Shao's mother was from the poor peasant class, they were allowed to return to their home.

Shao's experience of high school also differed from Yong's. Like Yong, she had a long trudge to and from her high school on weekends—six miles each way. She was also malnourished, though she had a marginally better diet that included such luxuries as eggs. Shao's ability to include eggs in her diet came after being diagnosed with anemia; the doctor prescribed more protein, which her mother found mostly in the form of eggs. Yong only received one egg per year on his birthday. Rather than eat it immediately, he secreted it away for later, enjoying the anticipation.

Unlike Shao, who was fortunate to have access to a doctor, Yong's only access to healthcare was the itinerant "barefoot doctor" who periodically visited his village and schools. Mao had launched the program to deliver at least minimal care to remote villages. Selected peasants were given basic first-aid instruction, a manual describing treatment for common ailments and accidents, and sent forth.

Like Yong, Shao was among the few in her middle school who passed the exam to enter high school. However, only one landlord class student from each of the four sections in her school could be recommended for high school entry. She was not selected despite her best efforts to perform as a committed and diligent member of the school and her village. Unlike Yong's father, however, Shao's father could fall back on *guanxi*. He contacted a friend in the country government who, in turn, contacted a friend who was a principal of a high school in their area, who admitted Shao.[68]

By contrast, Yong's family had no *guanxi* to call on in times of need. Both sides of the family were poor farmers, and everyone in his home village was profoundly poor. Yong, like those around him, was on his own. Rather than an impediment, this lack of social and political connections—like his small stature, poverty, lack of popularity, and marginal status—forced Yong to become self-reliant, self-directed, and resilient. If he was to continue his education, it would have to be on his wits and merits alone.

Shao's description of the *gaokao* parallels Yong's in broad detail. Both Yong and Shao took the examination over a three-day period. Both sat for exams in Chinese language and literature, political science, history, geography, chemistry, physics, and English. The cook at Shao's high school prepared special meals for the test-takers, "including *Yougao*, a small fried pie with sugar filling."[69] Yong was on his own to find something to eat at the restaurants in the county city where his examination was given.

Like Yong, Shao was among the fewer than 4 percent who passed the *gaokao*. Successful candidates then had to complete a form choosing from colleges that accepted students with their test scores. If they were not accepted by any of the three colleges they chose, they could agree to attend a college chosen for them by the provincial education department.[70] Shao's father suggested she include a medical college, a teacher college, and an agricultural college on the application to maximize her chances of getting a place.

Yong, on the other hand, had no one to advise him. No one in his family or village knew anything about college. He left his fate up to the district authorities who decided on placements. While Shao was accepted by an agricultural college, Yong hit another barrier: the medical physical required of all potential college students. Yong was judged to be too short and malnourished to attend college. He was told to eat better to improve his health and retake the *gaokao* the following year.

Undeterred, Yong and a friend, Huaming, approached the principal of another high school in the area where Huaming's family lived. The principal agreed to allow Yong and Huaming to attend classes at the high school to prepare for the *gaokao*. Huaming's family allowed Yong to live with them on weekends while attending the high school. The family was marginally better off than Yong's, which allowed him to improve his diet and grow taller and stronger. The next year he again passed the *gaokao* and, this time, the physical: Yong was deemed fit to attend college.

He was accepted at SFLI in Chongqing, which at that time offered a newly established two-year program in languages for prospective English teachers. His friend Huaming was also accepted into the program. Yong was expected to teach English in a middle or high school near his village after completing the program.

Reflections

Despite the turmoil of Mao's Great Cultural Revolution, Yong benefited from its educational reforms that prioritized schools in rural villages. The primary school, however poor, gave Yong the opportunity to discover his own interests and strengths. Despite its meager resources—a single teacher, no textbooks, no library, no music, no sports, no arts—the school exposed Yong to a world markedly different from his village. The school enabled Yong to feel that he was good at something, a feeling essential to his future success. For the budding scholar who eschewed the typical games and sports his peers prized, school was a refuge. The same holds true for many students today. Whether they seek shelter from family trauma, poverty, or some other life challenge, students benefit from a school that offers security, hope, and opportunity.

Schools should be sanctuaries for students, especially those who are from disadvantaged backgrounds. Many children living in poor communities are looking for a refuge. They want a place that offers possibilities, encourages their passions, and supports their pursuits. They are desperate for a place where they are recognized as beings with potential and can explore and discover their strength and talents.

Authors Robert D. Barr and Emily L. Gibson advocate for prioritizing students' unique talents and interests as an essential task of
schools seeking to cultivate a culture of hope:

> Schools can do much to help students find and develop
> their unique talents and interests through participation
> in school activities, clubs, and extracurricular activities.
> Nothing can match the effect of involvement in programs
> related to interests and talents on students' personal
> pride, positive attitudes, sense of belonging, and even
> school attendance (Damon, 2008). . . . The development
> of talents and interests can also provide the foundation
> for students discovering purpose in their lives and a life-
> long connection with others who share the same or simi-
> lar talents and interests.[71]

Students require more freedom and independence than most
schools offer. Children are natural dreamers and are capable of
accomplishing things beyond what schools can provide. Even in
the strictest schools, some students take risks to do what they wish.
This was Yong's experience—like other students, he had to take the
required courses that were typically taught by untrained teachers, yet
he figured out how to pursue his interests. This required walking a
fine line: following the mandatory school curriculum while veering
from the regimented, expected path. Even in this highly unfavorable
context, Yong was able to explore what he was interested in and develop
the skills and knowledge he needed to move on from his environment. This suggests that rather than forcing all students onto a
single path, schools, teachers, parents, and caregivers best serve students when they support them to find their own way. Yong's story
also demonstrates that defiance of authority and regimentation is
sometimes a vital part of students discovering their identities and
capabilities.

CHAPTER 3

The Traveler

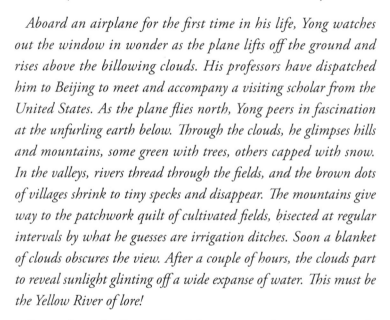

Aboard an airplane for the first time in his life, Yong watches out the window in wonder as the plane lifts off the ground and rises above the billowing clouds. His professors have dispatched him to Beijing to meet and accompany a visiting scholar from the United States. As the plane flies north, Yong peers in fascination at the unfurling earth below. Through the clouds, he glimpses hills and mountains, some green with trees, others capped with snow. In the valleys, rivers thread through the fields, and the brown dots of villages shrink to tiny specks and disappear. The mountains give way to the patchwork quilt of cultivated fields, bisected at regular intervals by what he guesses are irrigation ditches. Soon a blanket of clouds obscures the view. After a couple of hours, the clouds part to reveal sunlight glinting off a wide expanse of water. This must be the Yellow River of lore!

Rising from the Bayan Har Mountains in far west China, the great river winds nearly 3,500 miles through nine provinces, bringing its rich silt to the eastern plains before emptying into the Bohai Sea in Shandong Province. Yong knows well the story that the Yellow River Valley is the cradle of Chinese civilization.[72] Accounts of the river date as far back as the Xia Dynasty (2070–1600 BC), when Xia leaders dug canals to siphon off some of the flood waters that periodically devastated farms and villages along its banks.[73] Yong recalls that, more recently, a course change in the river played a role in the mid-19th century peasant revolt known as the Taiping Rebellion. Even more significantly, the drowning deaths of two million people in the fall floods of 1887 had undermined the Qing Dynasty's claim to its Mandate of Heaven, the divine right to rule held by China's kings and emperors.[74] This sad death toll pales in comparison to the nearly four million who died in the Yellow River flood of 1931, the deadliest flood in recorded history.[75] These tragedies convinced officials in the newly created PRC to invest heavily in flood-control projects, including the Three Gorges Dam on the Yangtze River. Despite the river's tragic history, Yong feels a thrill seeing it for the first time.

Although he is no longer the village boy whose world was limited to the immediate horizon, he has not yet comprehended how truly immense and beautiful the world is. Seeing the expanse of land stretching to the distant horizon fires his imagination and curiosity. Just as the land seems almost endless, so perhaps are the opportunities awaiting him. In a world so big, he feels he can find a place for himself and his ambitions. Three years studying at SFLI has widened his view of the world in ways he has never imagined possible. Now, he realizes how much more there is to see. The boy who mistrusted the residents of the next village has morphed into the young scholar who is eager to learn more about this bigger world and the people who inhabit it.

In this chapter, we see how Yong's time at SFLI offers him access to academic literature and enables him to cultivate connections with foreign faculty. These relationships open rare opportunities for him, such as accompanying a visiting scholar on a tour of Beijing and a subsequent trip to SFLI. The visiting scholar's demonstration of analytical software for desktop computers awakens Yong to the possibility of creating similar software for China. His involvement in an international research project offers an opportunity to do just that. In one year, he teaches himself enough programming and statistics to produce the first PC-based statistical analysis program. This accomplishment brings him recognition and acclaim from his professors and peers. It also opens the door to possibilities he never imagined.

Foreign Connections

SFLI was founded by the PLA in 1950 as the Russian Training Corps of Southwest University of Military and Political Sciences. Deng Xiaoping was one of the institution's founders.[76] By the time Yong arrived in 1982, it had been renamed Sichuan Foreign Language Institute and today is known as Sichuan International Studies University. As such, it is a well-known foreign language university, but in Yong's time, it was decidedly obscure.[77]

When residents of his village learned he had been accepted to college (a first for the village), they held a banquet in his honor. Villagers believed such an accomplishment foretold a future of enviable comfort and respect. Surely, Yong was destined to become a government official, the highest achievement they could imagine.

As he had done throughout his son's life, Yong's father placed his faith in his son and the path he had chosen. When it was time for Yong to travel to distant Chongqing to begin college, his father was at his side. Yong carried a bamboo basket with a few articles of clothing and a sheet that his father had made from bamboo. The 150-mile journey by foot, bus (over rutted country roads), and train from Yong's village to Chongqing took more than twelve hours.

Arriving at SFLI, Yong checked into his dormitory and found his room, furnished with eight narrow beds. Yong and his father were surprised to see cotton quilts on the bed slats. They had assumed that quilts were only for keeping warm, not to serve as mattresses. Yong spread out his thin bamboo sheet, reminded yet again of his poverty and how unlikely it was that he had arrived here. He understood that his father was proud and full of joy seeing his firstborn son on his way to a successful life, a life that was truly unimaginable for him.

Most of Yong's courses at SFLI were less than memorable. Historian Ezra Vogel describes the typical college experience this way: "Students of the 1980s using texts of the 1970s, taught by faculty from the 1960s."[78] But for Yong, the experience of being in a place that counted foreign teachers among its faculty and featured a library was invaluable. For the first time in his life, he met and conversed with people from not only outside his home province but also outside of China and had ready access to academic books and journals.

Also, for the first time in his life, he was in daily contact with people who were interested in ideas and a range of topics. His informal conversations with foreign faculty members helped him rapidly improve his English and exposed him to perspectives on China, the world, education, books, and more—ideas that were previously beyond his ken. The Western teachers he encountered were more knowledgeable than his Chinese teachers had been and enjoyed discussing ideas. They lived the kind of life that Yong longed to live, a life of the mind, rich in books, language, and conversations that had no purpose other than the pleasure of academic discourse.

Yong also discovered Xinhua Bookstore in Chongqing. Originally established as part of the CCP propaganda apparatus, the store's back room, forbidden to foreigners, housed pirated copies of foreign books, journals, and magazines. These covered a range of subjects, including anthropology, sociology, linguistics, psychology, history, and education. To get to the store from the SFLI campus required taking two different buses. Despite the distance, Yong visited each

Saturday or Sunday to spend the day reading. He read widely and randomly, choosing whatever caught his fancy. It mattered little that he only understood 20 to 30 percent of what he read. The information and ideas he could grasp fueled his desire to learn more. Yong also spent hours in SFLI's library, reading English magazines, journals, and books, an activity that did not interest his classmates.

His reading seeded his conversations with the foreign faculty at SFLI, who were, no doubt, eager to talk with their students. The foreign English teachers, who came from the United States, the United Kingdom, and Australia, lived in a special compound and were closely monitored. This was the early 1980s, and China had yet to widely welcome Westerners. They were, in the eyes of the Chinese authorities, not to be trusted. Yong, on the other hand, saw them as a source of valuable knowledge and information. He volunteered to accompany English faculty members on shopping or sightseeing trips, and he visited them in their apartments. On these occasions, he could ask questions that emerged from his wide-ranging reading. For the foreign faculty, the chance to discuss with a student something other than the weather and the price of pork in the market must have been a rare pleasure.

Because of his reading and interactions with the faculty, he improved his language skills far more quickly than his classmates did. One day, he wandered into what he discovered was an English-language listening competition at the college. On the spur of the moment, Yong decided to join the contest—and won by a margin of twenty points! In this case, as in others, Yong's knowledge and skill developed not from formal learning opportunities but rather through his curiosity, initiative, and appetite for discovery and learning.

Yong had a nose for learning opportunities and a willingness to seize them. Other students could have approached the foreign faculty, accompanied them shopping, and visited them in their apartments. But few of them did. Yong's confidence, eagerness to learn, and belief that he had nothing to lose served him well. If he mispronounced a word or didn't know the correct phrase, so what? He would learn. If a door was open a crack, he pushed right through it. Whatever was on the other side was unlikely to be worse than what Yong had already experienced.

During his second year in the program, Yong learned that the two-year program had been extended for a third year. This allowed him another year to read and converse with foreign faculty.

Beijing Tour

In his third year at SFLI, Yong took a course in pedagogy from a professor whose background was in Russian language. This is not as unusual as it may sound. Many Chinese engineers and academics had been trained in the USSR or had studied Russian in the 1950s when the USSR was China's closest ally.

HISTORICAL CONTEXT

On October 1, 1949, Chairman Mao Zedong formally proclaimed the founding of the PRC.[79] The following year, the Soviets and Chinese signed the Treaty of Friendship, Alliance, and Mutual Assistance. The terms of the treaty facilitated technical and cultural exchanges between the two countries.[80] The Soviets advised on everything from school and university curricula to railways, bridges, highways, and other infrastructure projects, taking part in more than 160 industrial projects in China.[81] As a result, Russian-language learning was required in some schools and in higher education. Thousands of Chinese teachers and technicians learned the language when they were sent to the USSR to study.

Few of Yong's peers took the course seriously. Pedagogy was considered a trivial subject and was scorned by serious academics. Yong, however, was deeply interested in the subject and sought out additional information from pirated Western books and journals. Yong's diligence and mastery of the course material impressed his professor.

The tasks entrusted to Yong testify to the faith that some key faculty members invested in him. For instance, the department chair of the Teacher Education Group sent him, while still an undergraduate, to Chengdu to pick up the department's first major personal computer—a 256 KB IBM PC (IBM 5150). This was the first affordable PC that IBM produced.[82] Soon after, his chair sent him to Beijing to escort a visiting statistics scholar from Miami University of Ohio and his wife. This was Yong's first time in an airplane, and it initiated him into the wider world.

Landing in Beijing, Yong was amazed at the imposing airport terminal, significantly larger than the one in Chongqing. He had never been inside such a huge building and worried about finding his guests among the throng of people scurrying through the airport's great hall. When the American visitors arrived, exhausted and pushing a trolley loaded with baggage, they spotted Yong holding a sign with their names. After quick introductions, Yong led them through the crowd to their taxi. He crammed their baggage into the trunk of the cab that took them to their hotel.

Over the next five days, he served as the guests' translator and impromptu tour guide as they visited the usual sights: the Great Wall, the Forbidden City, the Ming Tombs, and the Summer Palace. Because Yong had never visited these sights, he had researched them in advance to answer some of the visitors' questions. Conversing with the professor and his wife gave Yong yet another opportunity to improve his English.

Like other languages, English has peculiarities that confound learners. One of these is the prevalence of homonyms—words that are spelled and pronounced the same but have different meanings. Yong recalls how a common English homonym confused him one afternoon during their stay in Beijing. Yong announced that he had identified a restaurant reputed to serve exemplary local cuisine. The professor asked, "Do you have reservations?" Yong was momentarily confused. If he had reservations about the restaurant, why would he be recommending it? Only later did he learn that the word had at least three distinct meanings. Unsure of himself in the moment, he merely smiled and replied, "I'll meet you in the lobby at 5:00." The opportunity provided many such learning moments for Yong, which he navigated with his characteristic cleverness and initiative.

During their five-day sojourn in Beijing, Yong observed the visitors closely. He was keen to learn more about how they behaved and reacted to the environment. Western visitors were still rare and, to most Chinese, mysterious.

One incident during their visit to the Ming Tombs was particularly baffling to Yong. When the professor told him that he needed to use the restroom, Yong decided he would avail himself of the opportunity as well. Like most public bathrooms at the time, rather than individual urinals, the toilet was appointed with a metal trough into which water continually dripped. Users stood side-by-side at the trough to relieve themselves. As Yong stood beside the professor, he couldn't help but notice with surprise that his companion's urine was blue! Yong had been keenly aware of how different Westerners' customs, habits, and behaviors were. But he hadn't expected this. What was going on?

Later in life, Yong learned that several medications and dietary supplements can cause a person's urine to turn blue temporarily. But Yong didn't know that. Although the use of herbal medicines extends back millennia in China, dietary supplements were virtually unknown at that time. He was unaware of any traditional Chinese medicine that produced such a startling result. The experience left him confused, wondering if maybe Westerners were different in ways he had previously not imagined!

Their tour of Beijing's sights completed, Yong booked a sleeper for the three of them for the long train ride back to Chongqing. During the trip, the professor asked Yong to get him a Coke. Although Coca-Cola would eventually build bottling plants across China, a Coke was hard to come by in 1985.[83] Not wanting to disappoint his guest, Yong bribed one of the stewards to secure a bottle of the rare drink. Upon returning to SFLI, Yong found he had earned even more trust and respect from his department chair, who played a part in opening another opportunity for him.

Coding Success

In 1985, Yong's pedagogy professor was contacted about the possibility of SFLI participating in an international survey of students' English-language learning attitudes and motivation. He immediately thought of his star student as a potentially valuable contributor to the study. Yong did not hesitate to accept the offer to join the project, which he nicknamed the Chopsticks Circle Study because it included Japan, China, Taiwan, and Korea. Japanese scholars had created the project and took the lead. (Among the reasons that the Japanese were eager to include a Chinese university in the study was that the Japanese government was working hard to repair its relations with China and other Asian nations that the Japanese army had occupied during World War II.) Yong's English proficiency, trustworthiness, and intelligence made him an obvious choice. In addition, he had impressed both his pedagogy professor and the department chair with his competence and vision.

Vision was a key ingredient in Yong's success and a characteristic he shared with his father. Yong had a keen sense that if he worked hard enough, stayed true to himself, and was fortunate, opportunities that he couldn't foresee would open to him. He had often witnessed his father's determination to better his family's circumstances. If an enterprise didn't work out as he had hoped, he was undeterred. Other possibilities would be there. His vision of the world's many possibilities kept him moving forward. Yong shared this determination and optimism.

In his work with the Chopsticks project, Yong's vision of a better future intersected with the possibilities that the moment presented. The study involved collecting surveys from thousands of students in the four participating countries. The project leaders confronted a daunting problem: How would they analyze the huge amount of data they were collecting? Coding and analyzing the data by hand would take months, if not years. In China at the time, there were no computer programs available to complete such a task. Software was bundled with mainframe computers and was almost entirely confined to government research institutes.[84]

Yong had become aware of statistical programs through the presentations of the American professor he had accompanied to SFLI. When the visiting professor left, however, he'd taken the software with him. Yong recognized both an opportunity and a challenge. He had taken a course on computer technology and had learned the fundamentals of BASIC (Beginner's All-Purpose Symbolic Instruction Code), one of the earliest computer programming languages. Although his fellow students had not taken the course seriously, Yong had invested time and effort in learning everything he could about computer technology. The other English-language students couldn't see the relevance of the course to teaching English, but Yong was intensely interested in using computers to teach English.

At the same time, Yong recognized that if he was to analyze data collected for the Chopsticks study, he would need to know something about statistics. He discovered that the library at another university in Chongqing had a textbook on statistics on its shelves. He checked the book out and set about teaching himself statistics. This involved learning a vocabulary unlike the one he'd encountered in his English-language courses. Although he had always considered himself weak in mathematics, he found he could follow the logic of basic descriptive statistics. With an understanding of the concepts, the computations proved easier. Mastering statistics was, however, only part of the task that Yong had set for himself. Next, he had to write a computer program that would allow him to apply the statistics to the Chopsticks project data.

Yong threw himself into the task, fueled by both the scale of the challenge and the prospect of making sense out of a boatload of raw data the team was collecting. Some people get a rush from analyzing raw data—identifying patterns in seemingly random bits of information, drawing conclusions from apparently unrelated data, bringing order to chaos, and making sense of a slice of human behavior and beliefs. Yong literally worked day and night for a year, skipping meals, sleeping only three or four hours at a time.

Amazingly, by year's end, he had done it. Relying on his rapid mastery of BASIC, he had written one of the first, if not the first, Chinese programs that enabled statistical analysis of large data sets on a desktop computer. The lead professor and team members were astounded at his feat. As word got out about his accomplishment, Yong's stature on campus soared.

He used his newly developed programming skills for other projects of his own devising. Among these, he created the first Chinese game-based program for teaching English. For Yong, the real payoff was the satisfaction of having challenged himself and succeeded. Often, when he committed to a task, he didn't know at the outset whether he could pull it off. Challenging himself enabled him to test the limits of his abilities. That he managed to do it and do it well redoubled his belief in himself and his confidence in taking risks that others avoided. His success expanded the limits of what he knew he could do.

As often happens, an accomplishment of the magnitude of his data analysis program had repercussions later in life. This accomplishment subsequently shortened Yong's time to earn his PhD, helped him land his first faculty position, elevated his status within his profession, and set the stage for him to garner federal grants and the respect of his academic peers. Had his SFLI professors not invited Yong to join the Chopsticks project and had he not seized the opportunity, his life might have gone in a very different direction. Here, as elsewhere in Yong's life, Lewontin's observation about the role that chance plays in shaping our lives seems spot on.

In 1985, during Yong's third year at SFLI, he took advantage of another beneficial policy change. Anyone in his program could take the examination to continue to study for a fourth year to become a college instructor, as many colleges were looking for English instructors. Yong passed the exam and finished his program, graduating in 1986 with a four-year diploma and a bachelor's degree. His undergraduate thesis, completed in 1986, explored the feasibility of computer-assisted language learning in China. He was hired as an instructor at SFLI.

As improbable as it sounds, April of that year also saw China enact its first compulsory education law.[85] Momentum had been gathering since 1949 to ensure that rural children received at least nine years of education. This new law increased the demand for qualified teachers who would staff schools, especially in the poor, remote regions. To that end, the government created a program to send freshly minted teachers to be part of lecture teams that were dispatched to teach for a year in remote schools. Novice teachers could volunteer, as Yong did, or the institution would volunteer them. Yong was the sole true volunteer among a hundred teachers drafted from various institutions in the area. He was assigned to a community located a two-day journey by boat and bus from Chongqing. This marked not the end of Yong's education but a transition to a different stage in his life.

Reflections

Yong's experience at SFLI was shaped by several intersecting factors. His diligence, authentic love of learning, curiosity about the world, and determination to lean into challenges were all characteristics that allowed him to flourish during his college years. Many chance encounters and events shaped those years, too: the trip to Beijing with the visiting statistics professor, the Chopsticks project, and changes in educational policies. Yong had positioned himself for these opportunities and was ready when they unexpectedly arose.

Yong's experiences at SFLI also show the merits of learning for its own sake. Yong accepted the invitation to travel to Beijing to accompany the American professor not because it would help him with a future career objective but because he felt it was an intriguing opportunity. In the process, he learned a great deal about Beijing, American culture, computer-based statistics, and about himself and his capabilities. He took his pedagogy course seriously because he was interested in it, not because he knew it would help him achieve a future goal. Likewise, he proposed and developed the statistical software because he enjoyed the challenge of learning more about computers and statistics, not because he foresaw that this knowledge might look good on a résumé. Yet, unexpectedly, these opportunities he pursued out of authentic interest through which he learned new knowledge and skills turned out to be extremely valuable assets for his graduate studies and later life.

Learning for the sake of achieving some future goal is a narrow view of the purpose of education. If students are interested in learning something, they should be encouraged to do so. However, schools have a predetermined plan for students based on suppositions about what they will need to reach future goals. The plan forces students to focus almost exclusively on the state-mandated curricula and standards. Only rarely do schools enable and encourage students to learn knowledge and skills that interest them when they fall outside the required curriculum. The policy direction of the past several decades has been to narrow even further the traditional school curriculum.

Authors Doug Robertson and Jennifer Borgioli Binis suggest an alternative image—that of a "cardboard classroom" designed to help students identify and pursue their interests:

> This messy and imprecise space for iteration, failure, and learning is a cardboard classroom. Instead of a textbook-worthy explanation of a clear procedure, you see enthusiasm, vision, engagement, and learning. Instead of clean delineations between phases, you see jagged edges and rough-hewn solutions. It feels disorganized but hums along like a well-oiled machine. It looks frenetic but there's a clear sense of structure. Standards and goals are written in students' writing instead of put on the whiteboard by a teacher. The class likely sounds nothing like what your childhood classrooms sounded like, but you can't deny the joy and light filling the room.[86]

This image challenges the expectations of many educators and parents. At its core, however, such a learning environment comports with what we know about the diversity of students' interests, developmental trajectories, and motivations. Prejudging the value and consequences of different knowledge and skills can limit student potential. Status quo education may not appreciate the immediate and practical value of enabling students to pursue their interests and passions, but that doesn't mean they're not valuable. These, we contend, prepare students in unexpected ways for an uncertain future. Policymakers don't have a crystal ball to foretell how students' lives will unfold. The knowledge and skills that genuinely engage students may well be more valuable to them in the future than what is in the required curriculum.

In sum, as Yong's story illustrates, parents, caregivers, and teachers should encourage students to pursue their passions and interests and should provide them the necessary time and resources to do so. Schools should, whenever possible, create learning opportunities beyond the curriculum so that students can be exposed to more possibilities of learning and discovering where their talents and passions lie.

CHAPTER 4

The Entrepreneur

Yong sits on a weatherworn wooden bench as the boat carrying him and his hundred colleagues plows up the turbulent Wujiang River. The 170-mile trip down the Yangtze from Chongqing to Fuling, where the Wujiang flows into the Yangtze, was uneventful. The boat docked in Fuling the night before, as the river was too dangerous for night travel. Back on the river the next morning, the boat labors up the Wujiang, carrying Yong and his colleagues deep into Pengshui County, home to the Miao and Tujia ethnic minorities.

Yong watches the deep green hills and valleys on each side of the river. The boat engine whines as it labors against the racing current. In places, the river narrows as the banks close in and rise nearly vertically, creating dark green tunnels. Elsewhere, rice terraces climb the hills like a giant's staircase. Yong recalls that the Miao people are credited with initiating the cultivation of rice in China. Every few kilometers or so, he sees smoke rising from small huts with weathered tiled roofs crowded along the riverbank or tucked into valleys. In the distance, bamboo-hatted farmers, small and gaunt, wade behind black-backed buffalo pulling plows through rice paddies. Dusty roads snake their way up and down hillsides, twisting and turning with the terrain.

Much of this Yong finds familiar. These people are as poor as his own, dependent on rice, buffalo, and the vicissitudes of the weather. Yet, the countryside has a different feel. This intrigues him. He likes differences. They represent opportunities for discovery. They hint at perspectives that challenge his own. Yong is embarking on yet another adventure.

✦————————————————✦

In this chapter, we explore the valuable leadership lessons Yong gains as deputy team leader for the lecture team. During a routine return to SFLI, Yong learns of an opportunity that sends him chasing adventures in Hainan, designated a special economic zone. Operating as a translator, Yong forms influential social networks. This is thanks to his authenticity and lack of concern about gaining *face*—a preoccupation with amassing respect, honor, and social standing.

Leadership Lessons

As a volunteer for the lecture team, Yong committed to a year-long teaching assignment in the remote city of Qianjiang. The English journals and books he read at the Xinhua Bookstore and in the SFLI library had spurred his interest in education, and Yong saw this as an opportunity to experience education in another part of Sichuan Province. He also desired to help people who faced the same challenges that he and his family faced: disheartening poverty, food insecurity, powerlessness, and poor access to sound education. In joining the lecture team, he and his teammates were taking part in a policy tradition that stretched back to the 1950s: the Down to the Countryside Movement.[87]

HISTORICAL CONTEXT

From 1955 to 1980, more than sixteen million urban graduates, and even more rural school graduates, were sent to the remote rural and frontier areas of China to live and work like peasants.[88] The rationales for this rustication policy, officially called the Down to the Countryside Movement, were several: during the Great Leap Forward and the Cultural Revolution, educated youth were sent to the countryside to relieve some of the pressure on limited food supplies and labor markets in urban areas as well as to provide labor for farms struggling to meet government production quotas. Another motivation for the rustication policy was Mao's desire to create the next generation of revolutionaries to carry on the work of the generation that had fought the Civil War and established the PRC. A third reason was to disperse the Red Guards after they had served their purpose as the shock troops of the Cultural Revolution.[89]

The rustication policy had mixed results on all fronts—politically, ideologically, and economically. The "sent-down" often, but not always, clashed with the locals, who tended to view them as freeloaders whose paltry contributions to production in no way made up for the food they ate. Urban families whose children were sent down strongly disapproved of the program. At the same time, the sent-down youth became conduits for goods and equipment as well as ideas and information that spurred development in some rural areas.[90]

Despite the mixed results of Mao's rustication movement, policymakers of the next generation continued to believe that sending educated teachers to remote areas could benefit both the teachers and the locals. In 1978, Chinese communist leader Deng Xiaoping became the paramount leader of the PRC. Unlike Mao's initiatives, which sought above all to purify the Communist Party, Deng was primarily concerned with modernizing the Chinese economy.[91]

His economic and development goals required a well-educated cohort of engineers and technicians. Deng and his colleagues believed a meritocratic educational system was much more likely to yield the needed talent.[92] This required teachers who were well-prepared to identify and support students who had the necessary qualities of persistence, diligence, compliance, and content mastery. Deng's government recognized that the ability to speak English was also necessary to achieve the goals of modernization. To that end, by 1979, English had become a critical component of educational policy and was a required subject from middle school through higher education.[93]

Because English teaching and learning was denounced during the Cultural Revolution as the language of the oppressors, Chinese students during the 1950s and the Cultural Revolution entered higher education with little or no knowledge of the language.[94] Deng and his colleagues faced a double problem in staffing schools and higher education institutions: both quantity and quality. The low pay and status of the profession discouraged youth from pursuing teaching careers, and the teaching force inherited from the Maoist era lacked professional training. These were problems across the country, but they were particularly acute in remote rural areas. These needs plus the tradition of "sending down" educated youth to the countryside lay behind the creation of lecture teams.

In recognition of his initiative as the sole volunteer, the Sichuan Provincial Education Department appointed Yong deputy team leader. Each deputy team leader oversaw a team comprising ten to twenty teachers and reported to the team leader. This was the first time in his life Yong had been selected for a real leadership position. Although proud to have been recognized, he was also a bit apprehensive. Yong was meeting his team members, from his and other universities, for the first time. How would they respond to him as a leader? Luckily, as the deputy, he wasn't the decision maker; he was primarily responsible for communicating the team leader's decisions to the troops, listening to their needs and concerns, and reporting back to the leader. Despite his nerves, Yong was confident he would rise to the occasion as he had done before.

As the boat arrived at the dock in Pengshui, Yong noticed a line of buses waiting to transport each group to the cities to which they had been assigned. Yong joined his colleagues in boarding a dusty bus for the last leg of the journey to the city of Qianjiang, deep in the autonomous region of the Tujia and Miao people. Although Qianjiang is today a modern city, the city in which Yong and his colleagues arrived in 1987 was a dusty backwater. As the Chinese saying goes, it was a one-cigarette town: you could walk from one end to the other in the time it takes to smoke a cigarette.

The bus labored along the narrow road that wound through the mountains for several hours. When the group arrived, they stepped out into the cold September air to be met by the local leaders of the education commission and led to the dormitory where they would be staying. As a show of appreciation for the visiting teachers' services, the local education commission fed them three delicious meals a day throughout their one-year stay. Yong had the luxury of eating meat every day—still a rarity in rural communities.

Yong's students were adult English learners (ELs), teachers, and professionals from the city and surrounding area. They were taking courses on TV offered by the Chinese TV and Radio University, known today as Chinese Open University. Few of them had anything more than rudimentary formal training in English. Although Yong was not fluent in the language, he knew much more than his students did. In his classes were Miao and Tujia students, some of whom staffed schools that enrolled children from their ethnic groups.

Two events occurred in the following months that profoundly shaped the course of Yong's life. On National Day, October 1, Yong left Qianjiang to travel to Pengshui to greet a new group of teachers. As the teachers disembarked to stretch their legs and meet their deputy leader, Yong noticed a young woman whose beauty and demeanor attracted him immediately. He decided on the spot to get to know her; he had a hunch she could be the one. He introduced himself as the deputy leader and learned her name: Xi Chen. Thanks to this fateful and unplanned event, Yong had met his future girlfriend, the woman who would become his wife. Not for the last time, Lewontin's claim about the role of chance was borne out in Yong's life. Later he would wonder what would have happened had he not volunteered to go to Qianjiang.

Meanwhile, the team leader had returned to Chongqing, leaving Yong in charge. When the time came to decide where to assign the new arrivals, Yong used his newfound authority to send the men in the group to an outlying town, a place more dire than Qianjiang. Using the excuse that it could be a hardship for the women, he kept Xi and her friends in Qianjiang.

The second event resulted from his decision to return to Chongqing to register to take the graduate school entrance examination. After three months, Yong had become bored with life in this dismal city but left thinking he would return and fulfill his commitment. The only attraction of Qianjiang was Xi. They had started dating, an uncommon practice at the time, especially in rural areas. As they were outsiders to the area, the locals gave them a pass, assuming they were ignorant of prevailing customs. In addition, locals paid them a certain deference as educated city-folk. So, despite his boredom with Qianjiang, he left with the intention of returning.

Arriving in Chongqing after the overnight return trip down the Wujiang and up the Yangtze, Yong made his way back to SFLI. In his dormitory room, he found his roommate, Ke Chen, in an animated state. Yong had just begun describing his adventure to Qianjiang when Ke interrupted him, vibrating with excitement. Ke had learned of an exciting new opportunity thanks to Deng Xiaoping's most recent economic policies.

HISTORICAL CONTEXT

Deng's vision for the Chinese economy and modernization coincided with the rise and dominance of neoliberal economic policies worldwide.[95] International organizations such as the World Bank, the International Monetary Fund, the World Trade Organization, the European Bank for Reconstruction and Development, and others—along with Western leaders of the time such as U.S. President Ronald Reagan and UK Prime Minister Margaret Thatcher—touted the benefits of marketization and the privatization of state-held enterprises. It was in this international context that Deng's government consulted with Milton Friedman, godfather of neoliberal economic theory.[96]

To jump-start the economy, borrowing ideas from neoliberalism, Deng created four special economic zones in 1979, three in Guangdong Province and one in Fujian Province. The success of these zones encouraged the government to create additional zones, including Hainan Province in 1988. Formerly a part of Guangdong Province, Hainan had recently been designated a province in its own right.

As it had done for other SEZs, Beijing granted the Hainan SEZ exemption from export duties and significantly reduced tariffs on many imports. To encourage foreign investments, the government relaxed tax regulations and allowed investors to transfer their earnings out of China without paying individual income taxes. Foreign banks were allowed to open branches on the island and were permitted to open foreign exchange markets. In short, the

> government in Beijing created multiple inducements
> to make doing business and investing in Hainan as
> easy, attractive, and lucrative as possible.

Before Ke finished describing the opportunity in Hainan, Yong knew he wanted in, without knowing clearly what he was committing to. This was an opportunity to find out if a business career was for him. Ke told him, "We missed the Shenzhen miracle—let's not miss this one."[97] Any thought of registering for the graduate school examination took flight in a Shanghai minute. This was precisely the kind of adventure Yong liked: lots of unknowns, lots to learn, lots of chances to succeed (or fail), and the opportunity to experience a world heretofore unknown to him. The adventurous entrepreneurial spirit that had prompted Yong to sell sweet water to travelers and sweet potatoes at the town market awakened once again.

Adventures in Hainan

Hainan, at the time, was like many other boomtowns. People swarmed like ants through the streets, dodging every imaginable form of transport—bicycles, motorbikes, motorized rickshaws, taxis, cars, and buses. Foreigners in straw fedoras and linen suits ranged alongside the locals thronging the sidewalks. Street hawkers peddling drinks, fruit, trinkets, toys, and snacks called out to passersby, shouting at full volume to be heard above the din. The smell of cuttlefish, octopus, and other seafood roasting on grills permeated the heavy tropical air.

Freshly erected signs announced new restaurants, hotels, and teahouses. Men in suit jackets or shirtsleeves huddled around trestle tables, shelling and eating peanuts, drinking tea, and making deals. Construction cranes, cargo booms, and bamboo scaffolding punctured the sky in every direction. Several times a day, planes and ships disgorged yet more fortune-seekers from all corners: the Mainland,

Hong Kong, Singapore, Australia, the Middle East, Europe, and the United States.

This was China's new frontier that attracted multitudes of Chinese and foreigners intent on capitalizing on the relaxed regulations, potentially massive markets, and wide opportunities of the recently designated SEZ. Hainan wasn't completely lawless, but no one was entirely sure who was in charge or what the rules were, particularly foreigners who could neither read nor speak Mandarin or Cantonese. It was a made-to-order opportunity for a translation service.

Yong joined the throng of bicycles navigating the congested streets of Hainan. He pedaled hard and dodged vehicles and other bicycles; speed was of the essence. No doubt other would-be entrepreneurs had ideas similar to the one he and Ke had hatched. On his way to Hainan, Yong had stopped off in Guiyang, Guizhou, where he was joined by a friend who was teaching French at Guizhou Normal University and was also up for adventure. Along the way, others joined in too, including a guy from the Beijing Sport University who had learned English playing table tennis with international students.

Soon after arriving in Hainan, Yong and Ke went their separate ways and lost touch. (Later in life, they reconnected when Ke was a professor at the Central Academy of Drama.) By chance, Yong ran into another wannabe entrepreneur, Yi Feng, who had studied Japanese. Feng, who was older than Yong and came from Jiangxi Province, invited him to stay in the extra room in his apartment in Haikou, Hainan's capital. Soon, the two became friends. Recognizing their mutual interests and complementary linguistic talents, the new friends decided to start a translation business. As a base of operation, they occupied the lobby of one of the two international hotels and set up a couple of counters. Next, they printed business cards, *sine qua non* for doing business in Asia. As soon as he had picked up their cards from the printer, Yong pedaled through the crowded streets of Haikou, leaving their cards in hotels, restaurants, and teahouses that foreigners were likely to frequent. They got a few calls, and their business began to prosper. They worked long hours and lived austere lives, sharing the small rooms and subsisting on noodles and tea.

At the beginning, like most start-ups, the work was discouraging as they had to fight to build up a reputation. To gain trust and legitimacy, Yong and his partner initially took on whatever jobs came their way. Elders brought them old letters. Others brought contracts, leases, deeds, and other documents. Before long, though, Yong landed the first big contract. He bicycled out to a coconut milk factory at the edge of the city that was in the process of setting up new manufacturing machinery. Although commonplace today, coconut milk was unknown in China. The instructions for the machinery, imported from abroad, were in English. Yong landed a contract to translate the assembly and operating instructional manuals. The company, Coconut Palm Group, remains in Hainan to this day and is the largest producer of coconut milk in China. Whenever he sees people drinking the Coconut Palm milk, Yong feels some pride in knowing he contributed to the company's success.

During this time, Xi was rarely absent from his thoughts. He kept in touch with her back in Qianjiang as best he could, given the primitive state of telecommunications in China at the time. He sent her telegrams and, when he had the money, booked a long-distance call at the telephone exchange in Haikou. These calls were very expensive, involved a long wait at the exchange, and required coordinating with Xi to be at the exchange in Qianjiang when the call was scheduled. Separation had in no way diminished his love. He saw their separation as a test of the authenticity and depth of their feelings for each other. Their affection passed the test.

After two months, Yong's longing to be with Xi motivated him to return to Qianjiang for a visit. He left Haikou, with coconuts—an exotic item back in Sichuan—jammed into his bag, and made the three-day journey by train, boat, and bus. After a couple of days visiting with Xi, he returned to Chongqing, where he found a group of about ten faculty and staff at SFLI eager to join him on his return to Hainan. This did not sit well at all with the SFLI higher-ups. Their erstwhile exemplary graduate and volunteer was now *persona non grata*, an ingrate who was disrespecting his alma mater and luring away employees. They threatened to strip Yong of his position, kick him out of the university, and punish him. The threats had no effect; Yong returned to Hainan with an eager group of like-minded explorers in tow.

Many of the newly created companies hired Yong and his colleagues as temporary employees for a few weeks or months to provide person-to-person translation as well as to translate documents. These positions often came with political connections. One of the largest of these companies, Healthy China, had been founded by Deng Xiaoping's son, Deng Pufang. Deng's company was making a lot of money smuggling in cars, color televisions, and other contraband. The provincial government was still being organized, making it easy to evade any import duties or restrictions—especially if you were the leader's son.

Yong also served as a translator for the nascent provincial government's planning committee, providing translation at formal events and various meetings. As a twenty-two-year-old, he found himself mingling with high-ranking government officials and business leaders who praised his work. This surprised Yong, as he assumed there were others who were more competent than he. Gradually, he realized that maybe this wasn't the case. Among other clients was a delegation that included the U.S. Consulate General for Hong Kong, who hired him to translate for the visitors in meetings and at banquets. He accompanied the dignitaries as they visited businesses and factories around Haikou. Heady stuff for a young man. The English-speaking visitors complimented his translations, despite the occasional gaffe. For instance, he was unfamiliar with some English vocabulary such as *tourism*, a foreign concept for ordinary Chinese. He mistakenly and repeatedly translated this as *travel*.

Despite his illustrious connections and business success, Yong found the translation work increasingly less engaging. He was making a living, but he didn't like the work much. No longer an invigorating challenge, it became drudgery. Translating was a skilled trade, not true intellectual work. Moreover, he realized that he did not want to be a businessman. Amassing money, beyond what he needed to live, held no interest for him. The constant pressure and hustle to find and cultivate new clients was tiring, unsatisfying, and time-consuming. He realized he missed the life of the mind that being an academic afforded. He remembered how he'd wept as he packed books to take to Hainan during his return visit to Chongqing. The thought of abandoning the academic world for a life that drained him and didn't feed his spirit depressed him.

He thought more and more about how much he missed bookstores, libraries, academic articles and books, and opportunities to talk and explore ideas. Xi's year-long commitment to teach in Qianjiang would soon end, and she would return to Chongqing. He longed to return to her and SFLI, even if that meant ingesting a large bowl of crow. Having to face SFLI administrators after slighting them could be embarrassing. More importantly, a core Chinese belief is that a person should continually move forward and upward without looking back. Yet, none of this bothered Yong in the slightest. He told the university he would accept whatever punishment they meted out and cheerfully ate his serving of crow. SFLI cut his salary and put him on probation for a year, reserving the right to dismiss him without cause at any time.

Back at SFLI, Yong dove into his academic work with renewed zeal. He compiled textbooks and wrote articles that were quickly accepted and published. Dissatisfied with the standard fare assigned in English classes, usually literary classics such as Shakespeare's plays and *Tom Sawyer*, he assembled materials he gathered from pirated journals and academic books, like those he read in the Xinhua Bookstore and the SFLI library, to create his own textbook, *Readings in English for Education Majors*. When his colleagues saw what he was doing, they followed his lead and began creating their own textbooks as well. Yong was back where he belonged.

Authenticity and Face

In this period of Yong's life, he learned a lot about himself, particularly about his capabilities and the life he wanted. The Hainan adventure had been a particularly valuable experience. Yong now knew that whatever he undertook needed to feed his appetite for ideas, intellectual engagement, and learning. Business had not engaged the potential he recognized in himself. He learned that while he could succeed in business if he chose to do so, this type of success brought him little satisfaction, especially compared to the effort and time required.

The adventures in Hainan and Qianjiang also taught him that he had a capacity to lead others. His easygoing personality, humor, intelligence, and authenticity drew others to him; people trusted him. The absence of subterfuge and hidden agendas allowed those in his orbit to relax, drop their guard, and enjoy playful interactions with him. But Yong didn't hesitate to make decisions in his best interest even if he displeased others in the process, as happened when he left SFLI. Such honesty was rare in China's competitive culture. Yong summarizes this phenomenon in this observation: "We Chinese are vertically obedient and horizontally competitive." Opportunities are viewed as a zero-sum game: "For me to win, you must lose."

Yong drew people to him in large part because of his authenticity and his obvious comfort in his own skin. Author Susan Harter defines *authenticity* as "the ability to act in accord with one's true inner self."[98] Where does this authenticity come from? Harter posits that "people with true self-esteem exhibit greater integrity and authenticity because they do not base their self-worth on achieving goals established for the self by others."[99] This perfectly captures Yong's way of being in the world. All his life, he pursued goals that he established for himself. Others could sense his self-assurance, self-sufficiency, and self-esteem.

Authenticity seems closely related to the concept of face. Researcher David Ho defines *face* as:

> The respectability and/or deference which a person can claim for himself from others, by virtue of the relative position he occupies in his social network and the degree to which he is judged to have functioned adequately in that position as well as acceptably in his general conduct.[100]

Ho argues, contrary to common belief, that face is not a facet of personality nor merely an Asian phenomenon:

> The distinction which I have made between face on the one hand and personality and personal prestige on the other is a basic one with great theoretical import. It reflects two fundamentally different orientations in viewing human behavior: the Western orientation, with its preoccupation with the individual, and the Chinese orientation, which places the accent on the reciprocity of obligations, dependence, and esteem protection.[101]

Just as the absence of expectations for his actions and achievements freed Yong to pursue his own interests and plans, so too did his lack of concern about losing or gaining face. He was not worried about the position he occupied in his social network or the judgments of others. As others observed his behaviors and interactions, they realized that Yong spoke and acted without concerns about face.

As abjectly poor peasants, Yong's family lacked social standing and couldn't afford to devote thought or effort to social niceties such as face. They were fully occupied in figuring out where their next meal would come from.

Yong cared not at all how others esteemed him. When SFLI punished him for running off to Hainan without so much as a fare-thee-well, he wasn't embarrassed or humiliated. Growing up, he had experienced far worse. This lack of regard for face also freed him to undertake risky opportunities with little concern about possible failure. Yong was continually driven by a sense that he was capable of achieving whatever he determined to do. An inner fire burned in him that kept him moving forward.

Reflections

Some might regard volunteering to teach in Qianjiang and striking out for Hainan as detours from Yong's career path. They might wonder, "If Yong intended to become a scholar, why didn't he apply to graduate school and take the exam?" Instead, he left SFLI to teach as a volunteer and then dropped everything to try his hand at business. And yet, had he not volunteered to teach in Qianjiang, he wouldn't have met and fallen in love with Xi. Had he not rushed off to Hainan, he wouldn't have succeeded as a translator for high-level officials, thereby developing new skills and building his confidence. Perhaps most critically, he learned his true calling was as a scholar, not a businessman.

Although Western cultures valorize success stories, detours and setbacks can lead to growth, and failure is a powerful teacher.[102] Through sidetracks and missteps, sometimes big ones, we learn about ourselves, our talents, limitations, and passions.

Many educators promote "strengths-based" and "passion-driven" education. Yet, we are often ignorant of students' genuine strengths and passions. We create assessments in our attempt to identify these strengths and passions. However, it is through actual experiences that we and our students can recognize their talents and interests. Students need a wide array of experiences to try, fail, and ultimately succeed. Learning what they are not suited for and doesn't engage them is as important as discovering what they are suited for and interests them.

Perhaps supporting students to view failure as a normal part of learning begins with teachers committing to do the same. Author Peg Grafwallner writes about productive struggle in *Not Yet . . . And That's OK*, encouraging teachers to model a healthy relationship with mistakes:

> Toxic perceptions about failure being an endpoint make it paramount for teachers to be open to their own so-called failures in the course of instruction. When you experience a misstep in the classroom, model for students why that mistake is just a beginning. Instead of ignoring or covering up mistakes, immerse yourself in them and model for students how mistakes become a part of the learning process. By knowing there will be setbacks and obstacles, students can anticipate that the work they do will be hard and the task will be vigorous, but the essential productive struggle will lead to a satisfying accomplishment.[103]

If schools are to allow students the space to discover their passions and interests in an authentic way, they must strive to create a culture that normalizes failure and communicates that mistakes are pathways to learning.

In life, we may overplan. As John Lennon said, "Life is what happens to you while you're busy making other plans."[104] Youth is a precious time when teachers, parents, and caregivers should support students to try different things and encourage them to see mistakes as a vital part of the learning process. Only in retrospect can a person judge a particular undertaking to be a detour. Taking advantage of the opportunities we are given allows us to learn whether the path is one we wish to follow or another detour that allows us to learn and grow. Ultimately, detours and mistakes are necessary to understand ourselves and our options.

In deciding to go to Qianjiang and, later, Hainan, Yong didn't even entertain the possibility that these were mistakes or detours. He grew up among people who were too poor, risk-averse, or content with their lot to venture forth into the broader world. Yong's view, on the other hand, was: What do I have to lose? If the detours ended up being dead ends, so what? He would be no worse off than he already was.

As we see, throughout his life, Yong's desire to explore, risk failure, and strike out for both literal and metaphorical new territories drove his decisions. Some of us, when young, have a plan, a map that will guide us to a predetermined end. We know what trade or profession or calling we wish to pursue. Others of us just keep moving forward without a map or plan. Detours and missteps are part of the process. We have an almost-blind faith, streaked through with a layer of naïveté, that if a particular opportunity doesn't pan out, another will appear. Qianjiang and Hainan were such opportunities. And in both instances, twenty-one-year-old Yong didn't hesitate.

CHAPTER 5

The Breadwinner

Yong and Xi venture out to shop at the stalls in a nearby market. The day is bright, unusually warm and pleasant for January in Chongqing, when the temperature can dip into the low thirties. Shoppers swarm through the stalls as merchants shout out their wares and children play their games, laughing and squealing as they weave through the forest of adult legs.

Despite the pall cast by the suppression of the June Fourth demonstrations in Beijing and throughout the country, Yong feels optimistic. Two of his articles and a book have been published and are proving popular. And he has somehow managed to win the appreciation of the bright, knowledgeable, and attractive woman at his side.

On their way back from grocery shopping, Yong and Xi pass the office for marriage registration. Although they have not discussed the matter at length, they both understand that, someday soon, they are going to marry. Seeing the office, Yong thinks, Why not now?

Turning to Xi, he says, "We could go in and get our marriage license now. What do you think?"

"Why not?" she answers with a shy smile.

Shortly after, the newlyweds emerge with license in hand. True to character, they eschew any type of ceremony. They do, however, provide a hot pot dinner to which they invite their friends and relatives. Xi's parents are initially unsure about their new lowest-peasant-class son-in-law. Xi's father is a professor of Russian at SFLI, and her mother is college educated and a librarian at the university. By the standards of the time, they are middle-class urbanites. Is this young man worthy of their smart, lovely daughter? What prospects does he really have? In time, Yong will allay their concerns. They will grow to appreciate his talent and the care he takes of their daughter.

Chance has brought Yong an unexpected gift. He resolves to ensure that Xi's life with him will be as fulfilling and joyful as he can make it. A Chinese proverb captures, for Yong, his thoughts about his marriage: "A friend, one soul, two bodies."

In this chapter, we see how Deng Xiaoping's reforms exposed Chinese citizens to Western culture and sparked debate and demonstrations, especially on college campuses. During this time of enthusiastic engagement in political discourse and expressions of pent-up discontent, Yong's apartment becomes a salon of sorts, a place where faculty and students gather to discuss their country's future. After the tragic events in Tiananmen Square and the suppression of demonstrations elsewhere, Yong, like many of his compatriots, feels his prospects in China dimming. Through a chance friendship with a visiting American scholar, Yong turns his attention to the United States when Linfield College in Oregon invites him to visit.

The Salon of the Zhaos

As Yong was programming, writing, and teaching in 1988, China was entering a remarkable period of reform.

HISTORICAL CONTEXT

By 1980, Deng Xiaoping had consolidated his control over the CCP, and the government began attempting to undo some of the damage caused by the Great Leap Forward and the Cultural Revolution. His goal was to transform China from a planned economy to a market-driven economy within a generation. The SEZs were the starter fluid for Deng's plan to turbo-charge China's economic development.

After Deng consolidated power in 1980 and eased Mao's handpicked successor, Hua Guofeng, out of the picture, market-oriented reforms dominated the 1980s. The Party dissolved collective farms and allowed individual families to cultivate their own land. Individuals could also establish small businesses, and many rushed to do so as the Chinese entrepreneurial genius roused from its long slumber. Privately printed media were also permitted to publish, although criticism of the Party was muted as no one was quite sure how far they would be allowed to go.[105]

The mood began to change as urban Chinese enjoyed some of the benefits of modernization. Televisions, washing machines, motorbikes, cameras, and computers became much more available for those who could afford them. Avant-garde art appeared and was displayed in galleries and other public venues. The idea of self-expression entered the discourse of the times.[106] Educational opportunities also expanded, giving more families hope for the children's future.

Believing that education was crucial for driving toward economic and technological modernization, Deng sought to improve the intellectual capital of his country.[107] In addition to reviving the Chinese higher education system, Deng's government supported tens of thousands of students and scholars to study abroad in Western institutions and bring back the latest knowledge and technology to their homeland.

Between 1978 and 1991, over 170,000 Chinese students, with government support, traveled abroad to study.[108] In addition, several hundred delegations of Chinese educators and more than 2,500 scholars visited schools and universities in the West during this time.

In addition to returning with knowledge and skills, students, scholars, and educators brought back an appreciation of the freedoms afforded their counterparts in the West. Access to television increased exponentially as well during this period, further expanding Chinese citizens' exposure to Western culture and society. By the end of the 1980s, roughly two-thirds of Chinese had access to television, introducing viewers to a much larger world and glimpses of life in the West that often belied the Party's portrayal of working-class misery under capitalism.

As higher education enrollment surged and awareness of Western democracy's personal liberties spread, faculty and students challenged the limits of freedom of expression.[109] Campuses buzzed with discussions and debates about the future of the country. Renowned astrophysicist Fang Lizhi openly criticized the government, noting, "Not a single socialist country has succeeded since the end of World War II."[110] He urged students to take up the cause of democracy, and students across China answered the call, taking to the streets to protest corruption and cronyism in the government and demand greater freedom of expression.

Although the 1986–1987 protests were largely confined to students attending roughly 15 percent of the approximate one thousand universities,[111] dissatisfaction with the direction of the country was more widespread. Not surprisingly, Yong eagerly joined the conversations and became something of a leader and spokesperson for dissent on the SFLI campus. His honesty, forthrightness, insights, and humor won over not only his students and colleagues but also others from outside the university.

His small campus apartment became a place where faculty, students, and others gathered to talk politics and the future of China, a salon of sorts for local intellectuals. Many of those who came were at least a decade older than the twenty-two-year-old Yong. He found that he shared much in common with these older dissidents who had suffered through the Great Leap Forward and had been sent down to the countryside during the Cultural Revolution. Like him, they were less interested in grievances about the past and more interested in China's future.

In the spring of 1989, Yong joined others in demonstrations on the SFLI campus and the streets of Chongqing. The unrest that had been building for several years spilled out into the streets of Beijing, Shanghai, Nanjing, and other metropolitan areas as students publicly mourned the passing of Hu Yaobang. Hu was a chief architect of the economic reforms and advocate of liberalization who had been thrown out of the Party in 1987 because, his critics charged, he had failed to contain the student protests. To the students, he was a hero and symbolized the more open China for which they longed.

Students were also fed up with their lack of control over their lives. Not only did the government control their choice of majors but also the jobs they would fill upon graduation.[112] Previously forbidden, criticisms of the CCP spread and intensified, appearing in publications and, most famously, on "big-character posters" pasted to the famous Democracy Wall in Beijing and emulated around the country. However, unlike prior protests that were typically confined to intellectuals and students, the demonstrations in the spring of 1989 included workers, bureaucrats, educators, farmers, housewives, and professionals—a true multi-class movement.[113] This is what most alarmed the conservatives and old guard within the Party.

The students were one thing—doctors, lawyers, and mothers were another thing altogether.

For six weeks, massive pro-democracy demonstrations took place not only in Beijing but also in 340 other cities across China.[114] With the world watching in April and May of 1989, as many as 300,000 to 400,000 people demonstrated daily in Tiananmen Square.[115] Deng and most of the Party leadership agreed that it was necessary to declare martial law to control the situation. To their surprise, many of the people of Beijing rose up and thwarted efforts to move PLA troops into the city center by blocking roads, railways, and even subways.

Deng saw the challenge that the ongoing protest posed as a potentially existential threat to his and the Party's authority and the social and political stability he knew to be essential for his Four Modernizations. The last thing the country needed, Deng reasoned, was to return to the chaos of the Cultural Revolution. On June 3, he ordered that the troops do whatever necessary to clear Tiananmen Square. As the troops moved in and some began to fire into the crowd early on June 4, the protestors quickly dispersed. By 6:00 a.m., the last of the protestors abandoned the square.

Observers disagree about the death toll, with estimates ranging from 300 to 2,600 with several more thousand injured.[116] Another casualty of the crackdown for many was the sense of optimism and hope that had been building throughout the 1980s. The student leaders of the protests were arrested, their followers targeted, and CCP General Secretary Zhao Ziyang removed from office and placed under house arrest.

Around China, protestors went underground, returned to work, or went into exile. Many of the latter group fled through Hong Kong or Macau, and some made their way to the West. They fell back on the strategy of keeping the foreign media informed about human rights violations and political repression in their country.

Their hope was that the West—and the United States, specifically—would bring external economic and political pressure to bear on the Chinese government to release political prisoners and observe fundamental human rights.[117]

Deeply discouraged by the news that slowly leaked out from the events of June 4 and aware that authorities across the country were suppressing demonstrations and arresting protestors, Yong retreated to the mundanity of daily life—in his case, as a teacher and scholar. Those who had regularly visited Yong's apartment stopped coming, afraid to bring him unwanted attention as the political monitors on the SFLI campus kept a watchful eye on any student gatherings.

Yong delved more deeply into his scholarship, reading and writing far into the nights, and producing academic articles at a furious pace. The popularity of his publications continued to raise his profile, and he received increasing numbers of invitations to write for various journals. He also channeled significant energy into his teaching. His knowledge, humor, and openness made him very popular with students. Unlike his colleagues, he stayed long after his classes to talk with his students not only about the course but also about other, more personal issues as well. He empathized with his students, many of whom felt pressured and adrift with little guidance for their futures.

For his own reasons, Yong also felt pressured and uncertain about the future. Increasingly, he viewed SFLI as confining. He had gained a reputation as an exceptional scholar despite working at an obscure institution that offered him few intellectual challenges. Many of his colleagues seemed to be merely going through the motions, not engaged with ideas as Yong was. Most seemed content to teach their classes, return to their apartments, and write occasional opinion pieces published in largely obscure journals. Their interactions with students were limited to classes and, with colleagues, limited to formal meetings. He found them uninspired and uninspiring.

New Horizons

Yong increasingly felt that he was backed into a corner. Like many others, the suppression that followed June Fourth reinforced his sense that options for intellectuals in China were strictly constrained. For the time being, he carried on, alert for new opportunities. He continued his work on the Chopsticks project, and he continued to teach, read, write, and publish. By age twenty-four, he had already published one of the most widely read articles in China at that time, in one of the most prestigious academic journals. He was increasingly recognized as a prodigy, publishing more and more highly regarded articles than scholars twice, even three times, his age.

His sense of accomplishment was fleeting, though. Once he had completed an article or book or a new computer program, he was done with it. He didn't care for accolades and spurned celebrations. As always, he was keen to move on, explore, push boundaries, and test his mettle against whatever came his way. The more daunting the challenge, the more eager he was to take it on.

The newest change on the horizon was Yong's desire to marry his longtime girlfriend, Xi Chen, and provide a home for her. Recognizing that he couldn't bring his bride to the largely bare apartment, he determined to furnish it. Like other consumer goods, furniture was both scarce and expensive. His solution was to buy, scrounge, or steal wood and commission an amateur carpenter he found in the street near the university to build what he needed. Because he tended to make friends with nearly everyone he met— regardless of class, position, or age—Yong convinced the university security guards to help him forage for materials. In one instance, they even helped him pilfer a door from a garage on the campus to provide wood for a table.

Yong and Xi married on January 1, 1990. Xi's presence in his life helped to assuage some of the unrest he felt. Having someone with whom to laugh and share his thoughts and ideas made his dismay with his circumstances more than bearable. In September 1991, their life changed radically with the arrival of a son, Yechen. Yong's sense of responsibility for his family grew. Now, he needed to consider the impact of his decisions on both Xi and their son.

Opportunity presented itself once again in the form of a visiting scholar from the United States: educational psychologist Keith Campbell from Linfield College in Oregon. Yong and the young psychologist struck up a friendship and began working on a book together. Although they never finished the book, their collaboration resulted in an invitation for Yong to join the Linfield faculty as a visiting scholar. Accepting the offer would require Yong to be away from his wife and their newborn son, a prospect that made him hesitant to accept the offer. As he deliberated, Yong experienced a professional snub that decided the matter for him.

In 1990, the British Council announced plans to establish a testing center in Chongqing. Originally formed in the 1930s as the cultural outreach arm of the government, the British Council would eventually have a presence in over 100 countries. In addition to offering courses and cultural events, British Councils have also served as testing centers, particularly for the overseas Oxbridge and Cambridge English proficiency examinations. International students applying to UK universities are required to take these exams, which have been computer-based since the 1990s.

When the Chongqing British Council contacted SFLI as a potential local partner, Yong was the obvious candidate for the SFLI leadership to second to work on creating the new center. Afterall, he alone among the faculty was accomplished in both the English language and computer programming technology. Despite his qualifications and sterling recommendations from his professors, the SFLI president chose an older professor who was better connected and came from a higher social class. The radical equalitarianism, a hallmark of the Mao era, had clearly gone the way of the Little Red Book and Mao jackets.

By the early 1990s, pre-Mao social attitudes and prejudices were making a comeback. *Guanxi* was once again the currency of the sociopolitical arena. Of course, *guanxi* never disappeared but was merely hiding behind the thin veil of much ballyhooed equalitarianism. Despite his successes and his growing network of colleagues and friends, Yong lacked the generational *guanxi* that continued to benefit the few. *Plus ça change, plus c'est la même chose.*

The invitation to visit Linfield College arrived at just the right moment for Yong. His work on the Chopsticks project was wrapping up. The post-Tiananmen political atmosphere was nearly as oppressive as it had been in the Maoist era. The snub from the SFLI president had reminded him that, for all the lip service paid to the virtues and worthiness of the proletariat, *guanxi* and social class still ruled China. He also now had a family of his own to consider. Laboring as an assistant professor at an obscure provincial institution did not promise a prosperous future for his family. His success in teaching and publishing had assured him that he had the academic talent to succeed at any institution.

Plus, the United States held an allure for Yong. As more information and news flowed into China during the Deng era, he became aware of the opportunities widely available in the United States. U.S. citizens enjoyed freedom of expression, and Chinese émigrés were starting successful businesses and becoming wealthy. Most appealing to Yong was the freedom people seemed to have to choose their own paths, exercise their imaginations, and apply their skills and talents.

After discussing the opportunity with Xi, he decided to accept the invitation from Linfield and to take a leave of absence from his faculty position at SFLI. In September 1992, after obtaining his passport and visa, Yong made the taxing journey from Chongqing to

Hong Kong. He felt a mixture of emotions as the airplane ascended: excitement about what awaited him in Oregon, concerns about leaving his wife and newborn son, and uncertainty about what lay ahead.

Reflections

The period of Yong's life from 1988 to 1992 was marked by profound political and economic changes that shaped his view of life in China and his prospects as a scholar, husband, and father providing for his family.

Yong's personal attributes—specifically, authenticity, resistance to authority, likability, and vision—earned him the respect of his peers at a time when many Chinese were questioning authorities and the direction of their country. Chance had brought him to this moment in history, and his personality and temperament drew others to him who recognized his leadership qualities.

The brutal suppression of the June 4, 1989, uprising crushed the exhilarating hopes for reform. Against this backdrop, Yong's personal life changed dramatically as he married Xi and fathered Yechen, who was born on September 4, 1991. Dedicated more than ever to his scholarly pursuits, Yong was also dedicated to providing for his family. Throughout this time, he was keenly on the lookout for opportunities to improve his family's circumstances—just as his father had done. Through his scholarship and growing professional reputation as well as his work on the Chopsticks project, he had positioned himself for the next opportunity. Moreover, he had begun to envision possibilities that he could never have imagined before. For instance, the possibility for him and his family to leave Sichuan Province to explore the broader world had now emerged. Such a possibility would have been literally unimaginable for the young man who arrived in Chongqing for college a decade before—much less for the boy peddling sweet water two decades earlier.

In his exploration of what is possible to those who keep an open mind, Associate Professor Vlad Glăveanu writes:

> Most of the time we relate to the world, including to ourselves and other people, in a conventional and highly predictable manner. We use objects as they are "supposed" to be used, we interact with others as we are expected to, we think about our society in the way we know we should. The conventionality of such hegemonic, taken-for-granted perspectives or action orientations reinforces sameness (e.g., between the positions and views of self and other, between what we did yesterday, what we do today, and what we will do tomorrow). Such unquestioned conventionality of the perspectives we enact is what I equate with an absence or, at least, with a decline in our sense of the possible.[118]

Yong had acted unconventionally throughout his relatively short life. He had chosen to take school seriously when hardly anyone else in his context did. He had concentrated on literature and language when educational policy prioritized mathematics and science. He had bent or broken school rules when others reflexively complied. He had worked hard in his courses at SFLI while others did only the minimum. He had volunteered to teach in a remote city when his peers had to be conscripted to do so. He had openly dated the woman he loved when such behavior was generally considered immoral. He had opened his apartment to other dissidents when the campus *apparatchiks* were attempting to suppress dissent. His teaching and writing consistently challenged accepted educational dogma. Through these actions, Yong developed an understanding of the possible, consistently differentiating his sense of himself from those in his orbit and reframing conventions.

Glăveanu takes pains to distinguish between "new perspectives" and "the possible": "the possible is not equated here with a new perspective . . . but designates both the awareness and exploration of the space created by developing multiple instead of singular relations with the world."[119]

By the time he turned twenty-seven in 1992, Yong had created multiple relations with the world. Initially, he was a child of the village relating to his family and neighbors. Subsequently, through his education and his work in Hainan, he developed multiple other relations with individuals from a range of backgrounds and sociocultural contexts radically different from any he had previously experienced. As a key contributor to the Chopsticks project and a rising star in the academic firmament, he forged relations with students, colleagues, foreign scholars, and the wider world of scholarship. As a convener of animated conversations about reform and the future of his country, he created relationships with like-minded intellectuals and established a stance toward political authorities. As a husband and father, he created deeply emotional relations with his wife and son. These experiences served to dramatically reshape his understanding of "the possible."

Glăveanu describes it this way: "the possible is best conceived of as residing within *the encounter* between perspectives, as a space of emergence situated at the meeting point between person and world."[120] By 1992, Yong's experiences had situated him in a new space of the possible. Thus, when opportunities arose, he was ready to capitalize on them. He hadn't *created* the opportunities so much as he had been open to the possibility of the opportunities arising. As had happened for him numerous times before, a chance encounter served up an unexpected opportunity: an invitation to join the Linfield College faculty as a visiting scholar. When the door to the position at British Council was closed to him, he stepped through the next open door.

CHAPTER 6

The Global Citizen

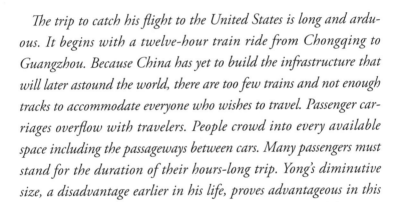

The trip to catch his flight to the United States is long and arduous. It begins with a twelve-hour train ride from Chongqing to Guangzhou. Because China has yet to build the infrastructure that will later astound the world, there are too few trains and not enough tracks to accommodate everyone who wishes to travel. Passenger carriages overflow with travelers. People crowd into every available space including the passageways between cars. Many passengers must stand for the duration of their hours-long trip. Yong's diminutive size, a disadvantage earlier in his life, proves advantageous in this instance as he is able to find space under some seats and sleep part of the journey.

From Guangzhou, he takes a bus to Shenzhen. Much like Hainan, Shenzhen is an SEZ, and a buzzing hive of activity. Workers from around the country pour in to help transform an erstwhile sleepy fishing town of 30,000 inhabitants into what will become China's version of Silicon Valley, home to more than twenty million people by 2022. A former classmate of Yong's invites him to sleep on the couch in her small apartment, and the next day, she helps him buy an inexpensive Western-style suit. He travels by bus to Kowloon's Kai Tak Airport that serves Hong Kong Island just across the bay.

Like Shenzhen, Hong Kong is undergoing rapid modernization, its skyline dotted with construction cranes in every direction.

After spending the night in the airport, Yong boards his United Airlines flight, amazed at the size of the Boeing 747. After the plane rises above the clouds, his mind wanders and a swirl of emotion rolls through him: excitement about what awaits him in Oregon, concern about leaving behind his wife and his one-year-old son, and uncertainty about what lies ahead. He is comforted to know that his in-laws in Chongqing will take care of Xi and the baby. Slowly, fatigue overtakes him, and he dozes off.

In this chapter, Yong's experience at Linfield greatly expands his view of education, technology, scholarship, and the world at large. He experiences some culture shock as he encounters phenomena unknown in China at the time: consumer choice, faculty's sense of responsibility for their students, and the degree of student autonomy were previously outside his ken. As he learns more about the lives of faculty at Linfield, he recognizes the possibility that he could succeed in higher education in the United States. After briefly returning to Chongqing, he is accepted into the graduate program in education at University of Illinois Urbana-Champaign. Returning to the United States in 1993, Yong and his Linfield friend Keith embark on a cross-country road trip that introduces Yong to the expansiveness and culture of the West and Midwest. In Urbana-Champaign, after facing challenges experienced by many international students at Big Ten universities, he dives into his coursework, teaching, and research assistantship, and begins to collaborate with his advisor and develop yet more software.

Culture Shock

Arriving in Seattle after his twelve-hour flight, Yong disembarked and navigated passport control before heading to baggage claim

---

and customs. Reviewing the Customs Declaration Form he had to fill out, Yong had a moment of panic when he realized he did, indeed, have an agricultural product—a small bag of the hot peppers of the type that gives Szechuan cuisine its reputation for spiciness. Looking about furtively, he managed to dispose of his contraband in a trash can before passing through customs unchallenged.

Yong emerged from the arrival terminal and anxiously scanned the waiting crowd. Spotting his Linfield friend Keith, he smiled and returned Keith's wave. He was relieved to see a familiar face after his grueling trip from Chongqing.

Carrying his suitcase and shoulder bag, Yong shook hands with his host and followed him out to a car. They headed south, stopping at a diner for a meal. Stepping out of the car, Yong inhaled an unfamiliar, almost sweet smell. He realized the smell was clean air. There were no low-grade diesel fumes, no small engine exhaust, no smoke from stoves burning sulfuric coal. Looking around in all directions, he saw clear skies. To the east, he even noticed distant mountains, a gray outline against the white clouds.

Inside the restaurant, Yong studied the menu. He was struck by the number of choices—there were so many items on the menu, and each item seemed to offer multiple options. If he wanted a hamburger, he could choose from bacon burgers, cheeseburgers, and pepper burgers. There was even a "Build Your Own" option—whatever that was. He scanned each item, marveling at the many choices. In the end, he asked his host to order something for him. He was unused to the experience of consumer choice.

HISTORICAL CONTEXT

Consumer choice did not exist in 20th century China. People took whatever was available—and felt fortunate to have even that. Perhaps two or three brands were available for commonplace items such as cigarettes, candy, beverages, and canned goods, but these were often produced by the same state-owned company. This began to change under Deng. For example, beginning in 1992, Deng allowed companies other than China Tobacco to manufacture cigarettes (although China Tobacco was, and remains, the most profitable company in China, accounting for 43 percent of cigarette sales worldwide). Coming from a poor remote province at the far end of the supply chain, Yong had yet to experience the gradual expansion of choices that wealthier residents in coastal urban areas were enjoying.

After lunch, they headed south on the I-5 expressway for the two-and-a-half-hour drive down to Portland, Oregon, where Keith had an apartment and where Yong lived for the next several months. Portland was less than an hour from Linfield College, which was located in the small town of McMinnville, Oregon.

As they traveled, Yong was surprised by the number, size, and cleanliness of the vehicles; the expanse and smoothness of the highway; and the lush greenness of the countryside. Not only were there many more cars—and more designs and models—than even in Beijing, but also all the drivers seemed to know what they were doing. They stayed in the clearly marked lanes, used signals to indicate lane changes and turns, and generally appeared to be following a common set of rules. Yong was astounded to see that some drivers were also drinking a beverage as they drove! Chinese drivers dared not take a hand off the wheel as they needed to be prepared for sudden movements from surrounding vehicles at any moment.

Eventually, Yong grew used to the new features of his environment and closed his eyes to rest. He couldn't help wondering what other surprises awaited him in this new and unfamiliar country.

The Linfield Experience

The Linfield visit allowed Yong maximum freedom to explore and learn. He observed classes, read widely in the library, and chatted with faculty and students. The knowledge he developed in the Chopsticks project proved invaluable as he informally provided desktop tech support to staff and some faculty. This allowed him to forge relationships throughout the education department and produced invitations to lunches and dinners in people's homes. Faculty also invited him to their offices for informal chats.

Yong marveled at the luxury and sense of responsibility to students that individual faculty offices represented. At SFLI, only the upper administration had offices. Why would professors need offices? No one expected that faculty would meet with students outside of class, and expectations for faculty scholarship were very low. You taught your classes; then you were done. If students had questions, they could sort them out among themselves. If faculty members wished to write, they could do this at home.

After he had been at Linfield for a couple of months, Yong was asked if he would like to teach an introductory educational psychology course. He didn't hesitate. This was an unexpected opportunity that would afford him a close-up look at U.S. students and college classes. And Linfield would even pay him a small stipend. He got a copy of the educational psychology textbook and read it through. He could do this. He encountered few ideas with which he was not already familiar. Although he had little formal study of educational psychology, he had read numerous articles and books from the field. In particular, he had learned a lot and even written about the psychology of language learning.

Yong's experience of teaching the educational psychology class made him appreciate the attitudes and dispositions of his American students and the informal atmosphere of the classroom. In China, students saw the teacher or professor as the infallible sentinel of all knowledge. Chinese students would no more have thought to question their professors than they would have thought to question the law of gravity. Students were taught not to question authorities of any type—teachers, parents, or officials. Chinese students had but one job: memorize the words of their professors and textbooks and reproduce them, *verbatim*, on exams.

On virtually any Chinese university campus to this day, students can be seen with a textbook in hand, their eyes closed and lips moving as they commit the text on the pages before them to memory. Their goal, whatever the intentions of their professors, is not learning in any long-term sense. Rather, it is to retain the information required to pass the exam. That 90 percent or more of this information will disappear from their short-term memory in a matter of weeks is of little concern. After all, they must make room for the next tranche of information they will need to memorize and store in short-term memory to pass the exam for the next class or level.

Many Chinese educators, parents, and political leaders recognize the limitations of their educational system. For many years, Chinese scholars have contributed to research literature on learning as a constructivist process mediated by the context in which learners mature. Changes have been made to the *gaokao* to encourage teachers to teach higher-level analytical and synthesizing skills. Yet, with a few exceptions, the pedagogy of yesteryear remains what most Chinese students experience today. Teachers and professors who may wish to adopt more engaging, interactive pedagogy face heavy odds. Class size (typically, forty or more students per class), parents' and administrators' narrow focus on exam results, and culturally embedded views of pedagogy and the purpose of education are formidable barriers to any teacher who might aspire to more creative practices. The pedagogy and student attitudes and behaviors Yong experienced at Linfield contrasted starkly with those he knew all too well.

HISTORICAL CONTEXT

The advent of the Deng Xiaoping economic reforms and the subsequent emergence of large private enterprises widened career opportunities for students beyond the realm of government positions.[121] Private sector jobs in prestigious companies such as Alibaba, Media, JD Group, Tencent, and Huawei are viewed as almost as desirable as government jobs, although they don't offer the same level of job security. Many graduates of top universities continue to compete for the lower-paying but more secure and often less-demanding civil service jobs. In 2020, nearly a million exam-takers competed for a mere 25,700 government positions.[122]

In other words, the goal of education has remained consistent over two millennia: for the state, to sort and select students who have the qualities needed to be competent and compliant bureaucrats and who will loyally serve the ruler effectively and diligently. For students, the goal is to successfully pass the required exams to advance in the system and, ultimately, attend a top university that would secure them a position of authority and comfort in either the government or business.

Yong had never embraced these obdurate views of teaching and learning. He had learned early in his school career that he could teach himself what he wanted to know and that texts were not sacred. They could be criticized and interrogated. Another human being such as himself had written whatever was on the page. If one human wrote it, another could challenge or refute it. This view was reinforced when he began reading and writing scholarly articles himself. As he read articles written by other scholars, he noticed many cases where authors made assertions or claims for which they presented dubious evidence—or no evidence at all. This understanding freed him to challenge orthodox claims. In addition, his experiences as a teacher convinced him that he could create relationships with his students that enabled more open and productive interactions. In these matters of teaching and learning, he was highly unconventional, as he was in nearly all matters.

The physical organization of classrooms at Linfield also impressed Yong. In China, student desks in orderly rows typified classrooms. The teacher assigned students to their seats, sometimes based on their exam performance. They expected students to sit silently erect, close to the front edge of their seats, eyes unwaveringly fixed on the teacher and the chalkboard. Classrooms at Linfield featured desks that could be arranged in multiple configurations. Because of the small class sizes, students frequently sat in a circle with the professor. This promoted informality and dialogue that Yong found completely novel and intellectually generative. Professors encouraged students to express their opinions, debate ideas, and raise questions. Rather than criticize their ideas and shame students for their lack of knowledge, professors encouraged students to develop and amplify their ideas. Of course, not all professors behaved in this way, but Yong observed the dynamic often enough to know that these were not one-off exceptions. In fact, stand-and-deliver, teacher-centered classrooms were the norm in the United States at the time.[123]

Being able to engage his students in conversations, probe their thinking, debate issues, and respond to their questions in depth further invigorated Yong's interest in teaching. He realized that formal education need not be the dull, soul-squelching experience that was so common in China at that time. Students could join their professors in analyzing and evaluating information and ideas. New understandings and ideas could arise from such exchanges. Rather than an endless grind of cram-and-exam, learning could be enlivening.

Yong recognized that the view of knowledge, learning, and teaching he was experiencing at Linfield was almost perfectly aligned with

his own. In China, his views made him unconventional, an outlier, an anomaly. At Linfield, the faculty held views of teaching and
learning that were like his. This encouraged him. As Yong interacted
with the professors and learned about their paths to positions in
the academy, he nurtured the idea that he could do what they had
done: he could attend and succeed in a doctoral program. Perhaps
his true intellectual and professional path was not in China but in
the United States.

He began to research graduate programs in the United States and
asked his friends on the Linfield faculty to suggest possible universities. He took the Test of English as a Foreign Language (TOEFL)
and Graduate Record Examination (GRE) standardized exams and
scored well on both (except for the quantitative part of the GRE),
and he submitted applications for graduate studies to several universities. However, as much as he enjoyed his time at Linfield, he
was also eager to return to Chongqing. He missed his wife and
son. Yong left the United States in the spring of 1993, anticipating
that he would return—perhaps as early as the fall—to begin his
graduate studies.

Shortly after he returned to Chongqing, Yong received news that
he had been accepted into the graduate program in educational
psychology with a minor in second-language acquisition at the
University of Illinois Urbana-Champaign. In fact, this was the only
institution that accepted him. Yong was delighted to receive the
admission letter: UIUC had been his first choice.

For Yong and Xi, the decision to leave China and take their
chances in a country about which they knew relatively little was
very risky. Yong recognized his Linfield experience provided only
a glimpse through a small window into a large and diverse country. Many unknowns remained. How would they be received? How
would they manage in a country whose systems (government, education, health, economy, and so on) were completely unfamiliar and

would be very different from those they were accustomed to? Where would they live? How would they earn money?

For Xi, the move would mean leaving her career. She was a professor and assistant chair at the SFLI Russian department. She had a comfortable job and a bright future. It would also mean leaving behind her parents and other members of her extended family. She had relied on them more than ever while Yong was in the United States. Yechen was reaching the age where he was bonding with his grandparents, who doted on him and whose lives were enriched by his presence. Besides her time in Qianjiang, Xi had spent most of her life in Chongqing, in and around the SFLI campus where both her parents worked. The prospect of moving to the other side of the world was daunting. She knew Yong would be busy with his studies, and she worried about being alone in a place where she knew no one.

At the same time, they were excited at the prospect of experiencing a world about which they knew little. The same sense of adventure, of challenging personal boundaries, of the potential for exploration and discovery that had prompted Yong to go to Qianjiang, Hainan, and Linfield urged him on. He and Xi made the difficult but practical decision that he should go to the United States alone and, once settled and oriented to the university and community, he would arrange for Xi and Yechen to join him following his first year at UIUC.

Midwest Road Trip

In 1993, Yong once again took the train to Guangzhou and bus to Shenzhen and the ferry to Hong Kong to catch a flight to Seattle. He remembered to leave the peppers in Sichuan this time. His friend Keith met him and picked him up, and they drove down to Portland. Keith had taken a job in St. Louis and was preparing to drive to the Midwest. Yong loaded his few possessions—mostly books—into his friend's car, and they took off.

For Yong, the four-day journey was a revelation. The trip through the snow-capped Rockies was, at points, breathtaking. Whenever they stopped, he reveled in the crisp mountain air and filled his lungs to bursting. As they traveled eastward, the greenness of the west side of the Rockies gave way to the spare beauty of the high plateaus and hills in southern Idaho and northern Utah. The openness of the land and the scarcity of towns and homes took him by surprise. This was so unlike the Northwest, especially the part of Oregon he knew. He thought of how much of this region was uninhabited. Sure, some of it was under cultivation. But most of it seemed wild, untamed, vacant.

As they drove through Salt Lake City, Keith pointed out the spires of the Mormon Temple. Yong had read about the Mormon community and faith, Joseph Smith, and the angel Moroni. As he'd investigated religions further, he learned that the Prophet Mohammed also encountered an angel that dictated what became Islam's sacred text, and Moses had returned from a trek up a mountain with tablets bearing the words of God. Clearly, this was a theme that major religions seemed to share. Chinese history also featured religious leaders who claimed to have had visions of the divine and to have a special relationship with God. As the Mormons were settling in Utah, a poor, failed civil-service examination taker, Hong Xiuquan, was building a following in China. Hong claimed that he had sojourned for a time in heaven, and subsequently, as he learned more about Christianity from missionaries who were flooding into China in the wake of the Treaty of Nanjing, realized his true identity was as the son of God and the younger brother of Jesus. Hong soon attracted as many as 30,000 followers, mostly illiterate peasants from the Hakka minority.[124]

Yong understood that Mormons would likely be deeply offended by being compared to Hong and his followers. Yet, he wondered what made Joseph Smith's, or Mohammed's, claims more credible than Hong's? He asked his friend if those who believed the Joseph Smith story tended to be superstitious and uneducated. He was thinking of the people in his village who were prey to ghost stories, superstitions, and belief in supernatural beings. He was surprised to learn that most Mormons were well-educated, and many were very prosperous.

Not for the first time did Yong remark on the disconnect he saw between being educated, being schooled in science, being encouraged to question unsubstantiated claims, and believing in the supernatural. Never having been exposed to religion, he had difficulty reconciling the idea of blind faith in anything or anyone—whether supernatural beings or political ideologies or religions or leaders or institutions—with the fundamental need for rational thinking. After all, it was science that had ended the scourge of smallpox, diphtheria, cholera, polio, and other illnesses. It was science that enabled the construction of dams in China to save the lives of millions from catastrophic floods. Science had made modern travel and communication possible and dramatically increased crop yields, saving even more lives. Science—not faith or unquestioned belief—was responsible for these innovations that had made the world a better place for billions. That science also created the bombs that destroyed Hiroshima and Nagasaki didn't, in his mind, negate the billions of lives it had saved and continued to save.

Again, what others may have regarded as a disadvantage was, for Yong, a strength. Unlike believers of almost any faith or ideology, he was not tethered to any belief system. He didn't assume that his way of thinking was inherently superior to any others. All humans were capable of exercising their rational minds as he did. He was also struck by the assumption that religions had a monopoly on morals and ethics. To assume that belief in some religious dogma was necessary for having a moral compass and behaving ethically seemed counterfactual to Yong. He knew that across history, ethical codes espoused by different religions had been bent to the benefit of the powerful and used as weapons of violence. He also knew that people who espoused no religion, ideology, or particular ethical code were often committed to and had succeeded in making the world a better place.

As they left the Mormon Temple in the rearview mirror, Yong and his friend also left behind the mountains and began their trek across the northern Great Plains. Just as Yong had found the Rockies awe-inspiring, the vastness of the plains was equally impressive. Driving through Wyoming, he saw fields of grain and corn that stretched to the horizon. For hundreds of miles, the landscape changed little, and Yong continued to wonder at how sparsely populated the land seemed to be. Farmhouses with multiple outbuildings and corrals and farm machinery of various types appeared at intervals. Grain elevators rose out of the fields like watchtowers. And tiny towns consisting of little more than a gas station, a liquor store, and a church also popped up. But they traveled for miles without seeing a human-made structure. Crossing the Platte River, they hit a one hundred–mile stretch of highway that was as straight as a guitar string before reaching Lincoln and heading northeast to Omaha, where they overnighted.

The next day, the drive through Iowa featured long stretches of highway that appeared to disappear over the ever-receding horizon. Gradually, the population grew denser, and towns and cities grew larger as they headed east. Yong began to get excited when he realized they would reach Urbana-Champaign that day. At the same time, he would have happily continued the trip. He was exhilarated by what he had seen and appreciated this rare opportunity to experience such a wide swath of the country. Keith dropped him off at the dorm where he was temporarily staying, bid him goodbye, and headed off for St. Louis.

Welcome to the Big Ten

Yong's first impression of UIUC was of its size and cleanliness. After settling into his digs in a dormitory the university had reserved for newly enrolled international students, he wandered the campus. He marveled at the tall leafy trees towering over the paved walkways and the sweet scent of freshly cut grass. Large multistory brick buildings occupied much of the campus. Eventually, he passed a building that was the size of a city block. On closer inspection, he discovered this was the library where he was destined to spend hours reading books on multiple subjects. Because he hadn't yet registered, he couldn't enter. Instead, he just stood on the steps taking in the building and gazing across the campus.

Later in the week, he registered and received his ID card. He also met with his advisor, Gary Cziko, who described the process of registering for courses. With a list of the agreed-on courses in hand, he entered the Armory Building, where long lines of students waited to register for courses.

Like the other students, Yong carried the inch-thick Catalog of Courses that his advisor had given him. He had leafed through the book, astounded at the variety of courses offered. Many of the titles intrigued him, and he wondered how many he could take in his time at UIUC. At SFLI, students had no choice in the matter. They were assigned a series of required courses. The idea of electives simply did not exist. The notion that you would take courses or even read books outside your assigned field was totally foreign. Yong had also learned from his advisor that as long as he took the courses needed to fulfill the requirements of a master's degree, he could take any other course in the university he chose if space was available. With his advisor's help, he successfully petitioned to have his prior work on the Chopsticks project fulfill his statistics and research methodology requirements. Still, he had to meet the guidelines for his master's program that were broad enough to allow him to choose from a list of approved courses.

Yong joined the educational psychology line, having no idea the process would take several hours. He surmised that students often had to adjust their program of studies on the fly as they learned that the courses they hoped to take had closed because the maximum number of students allowed had been reached. For Yong, the scene was surreal: the huge building with its military accoutrements; the hundreds of students waiting in long lines or milling about, some in a state of near panic, some sitting on the floor along the walls thumbing through the course catalog, and some rushing to embrace friends not seen since spring; and the atmosphere of excitement mixed with uncertainty and impatience. Yong had never experienced anything like this. Was this the downside of choice, a sort of controlled chaos? A few other students whose skin color or dress suggested they might also be international students looked on with bewilderment. He wasn't the only one who found the scene confusing.

Another unique experience arose when Yong met his short-term roommate, who was from India. Yong had never before spoken with someone of Indian heritage. He was deeply puzzled when his roommate rubbed shampoo into his hair before going outside. The roommate explained that he was using the shampoo in lieu of hair oil. Where he came from, people typically oiled their hair before going out or going to bed—a tradition that stretched back thousands of years. Yong was also intrigued by the way his roommate talked knowingly about other topics on which he knew very little. For instance, the student talked about illegal drugs—marijuana, LSD, and cocaine. Yong discovered these were common subjects of conversation at UIUC, but which he knew very little about and hadn't discussed with his friends at Linfield. Not for the last time Yong realized how limited his experience of the broader world was.

Linfield and his cross-country trip, however mind-expanding, represented only a razor-thin slice of human diversity.

Before long, the logistics of Yong's life on campus began to come together. With very little money, Yong was fortunate to receive a teaching assistantship for introductory statistics. He also landed a job as tech support in the College of Education computer lab. Thus, his work on the Chopsticks project had not only allowed him to comp out of required statistics and technology courses but also landed him jobs that, however low the pay, enabled him to support himself. He found a studio apartment near campus that was also close to a grocery store that catered to UIUC students. He had just enough money to buy a Macintosh computer.

Nothing at UIUC impressed him more than the library. The reading room reminded him of a church he had visited with its high ceiling and arched windows. Along the walls were beautifully built wooden bookcases filled with books, and two rows of long tables with chairs extended the length of the space that seemed as big as a soccer field. For a curious autodidact such as Yong, this seemed like heaven. The smell of aging books that filled the air evoked endless possibilities, ideas, and information to be uncovered. Equally amazing were the services the library offered, which included both knowledgeable and helpful staff and the convenience of requesting books and having them delivered.

Yong was eager to get on with his degree work and to take as many courses as he could manage within the limits the graduate school set. To these ends, he typically took four courses each semester, whereas the normal student load was two or three courses. He also managed to convince his professors to allow him to write a single integrative paper that synthesized ideas from all the courses he was taking rather than papers for each course. He used the opportunity his work in the computer center offered to learn about the newest technology, the World Wide Web. He learned and began to teach the HyperText Markup Language (HTML) for those interested in creating webpages.

His expanding computer skills also proved valuable in his work with his advisor. Cziko, a second-language-acquisition scholar at UIUC, was a well-known promoter of perceptual control theory (PCT), a philosophical theory about the relationship between behaviors and perception.[125] Over time, Cziko had created an expanding LISTSERV (an early email distribution list) of other scholars interested in PCT. The chain of email messages had grown lengthy and cumbersome. Yong and Cziko arrived at a solution: convert the LISTSERV into a website to preserve and allow easier access to contributors' comments. (Visit http://pctweb.org/lead/cziko.html to see the website.)

Later, Yong also collaborated with Cziko on an article in which they applied PCT to better understand teachers' response to educational technology.[126] As a byproduct of his work to develop the PCT website, Yong created a HyperCard program to convert emails into websites and organize the emails into threaded discussions. The program proved popular until other programs eclipsed it as both software and hardware grew more powerful and user-friendly.

As if these weren't enough to keep him busy, Yong also started a web-based online journal, Exchange. The website enabled English learners from around the world to submit articles and news reports. He invited doctoral students in the College of Education to help the contributors improve their English writing skills. This anticipated the advent of digital mass media as contributors were encouraged to write about news and events in their locale. At the same time, it served the educational purpose of helping ELs improve their written English and gave doctoral students experience working with ELs. This was all occurring in 1993–1994 when the web was in its infancy. Yong foresaw the educational possibilities of the web when few around him did.

As the year progressed, Yong found that his interactions with faculty at Linfield and his scholarly success at SFLI engendered in him the confidence to interact with UIUC faculty as an equal. This enabled him to have conversations with faculty that were more collegial than deferential. Like Yong, they were always keen to talk about ideas. They were also interested in his experiences in China as they knew little about the country. In fact, few had any international experiences at all.

The College of Education faculty who interacted with Yong came to appreciate his curiosity and knowledge as well as his accomplishments and scholarly potential. He also began to help some of his professors write grant proposals with the hope that he could get support as a research assistant if successful. Because of his interactions with faculty, he received their strong support when applying for jobs. Yong later discovered one of the best-known scholars at the College of Education, Dick Anderson, wrote a glowing letter of support that would help him land his first tenure-track position, at Michigan State University.

Reflections

Throughout his life, Yong has always been leaving old places for new ones. He left his village to attend school in another village. He left to attend middle school in a nearby town and again to attend high school in an even bigger town. Later, he left his village for college in Chongqing. He left Chongqing to travel to the United States. Every move has meant leaving a community of friends behind. Every move has meant leaving behind the familiar and known. Every move has brought with it a sense of no-going-back.

Of course, the no-going-back is not literally true. Yong has returned to China and his village many times. Rather, the constricted world that is his village and the constrained perspectives of his family and friends can never satisfy his intellectual restlessness and curiosity. He understands that his contrarian nature and drive to continue learning make him incompatible with much about Chinese culture and political context. He still loves the food, humor, affability, hospitality, and ingenuity of the people. When he returns, he enjoys spending evenings with old friends, drinking *baijiu* (a Chinese hard liquor), savoring each new dish as it arrives, telling stories, and joking, laughing, and (although he knows better) smoking as his friends do. These are good-hearted people who enjoy one another's company. Yet, despite these pleasures, he cannot see himself returning as some Chinese do after they have made good in the United States to spend their golden years in the comfort and familiarity of the communities they left. Becoming a global citizen had changed him in profound ways that called him to keep moving forward.

Yong's experiences at Linfield and UIUC reflect an adventurous spirit that has accompanied him throughout his life. He does not want to be defined by the status quo and is always seeking to go beyond what is defined and what is predetermined and pre-planned. Regardless of his situation, he can always come up with something new and dedicate himself to exploring the possible, which brings even more new opportunities.

He pursued adventure at Linfield by going well beyond the activities typical of visiting scholars. Unlike numerous visiting Chinese scholars at U.S. institutions who would observe classes and have meetings with faculty, Yong offered technology support, helped the department's nascent internet access, and even taught classes—none of which had been planned when he arrived at Linfield. He was not necessarily an expert in these enterprises at the outset, but he dove in and soon became an expert.

His teaching and technology experiences at Linfield paved the way for his assistantships at UIUC. Besides statistics, he taught a section of the educational psychology course for undergraduates. But the assistantships did not define him or confine him. He took the opportunities to do more. Not only did he manage the computer lab, but he also ventured into creating websites. He became an expert in building a website and taught HTML.

This was not all. Yong negotiated course assignments with his professors, taking on a lot more than a typical graduate student would do. He expanded the idea of web-based learning and designed software, neither of which was a course requirement.

This spirit of seeking adventures can only work in conducive environments. Yong was lucky to meet very open-minded faculty at both Linfield and UIUC. The Linfield education faculty, particularly his host Keith Campbell, not only allowed him to play with the technology but also invited him to teach a class. The UIUC faculty, especially his advisor Gary Cziko, were very open-minded and supported Yong taking courses outside the College of Education. They waived the statistical and methodological block of required courses. They allowed him to take a job thousands of miles away while writing his dissertation. All these made it possible for Yong to finish his PhD in just two years, during one of which he worked full time at Willamette University in Oregon and Hamilton College and Colgate University in New York.

Yong's eagerness to venture into the uncertain and unknown led him into exciting opportunities. His experiences with an emerging technology, the internet, were an excellent example of exploring the unknown for opportunities. In 1992, few were aware of this new technology, but Yong found it fascinating. He began exploring it, not because he thought it would lead to something in the future, but because he simply was interested. He continued to pursue this interest at UIUC, where one of the first graphic web browsers, Mosaic, was developed and released in 1993. Eventually, this technology shaped Yong's early professional life in the United States, even though he went to UIUC to study educational psychology and second-language acquisition.

But his pursuit of internet technology required a conducive environment, a flexible and open environment. Without this, Yong's adventurous spirit could have easily been stifled and could have caused him trouble. School curricula tend to be rigid and requirements stringent and inflexible. This often prevents students from exploring new possibilities and alternative pathways. Many families also have numerous requirements and rules that discourage children from adventures and explorations. Greater flexibility in traditional arrangements for children as well as adult support and encouragement are essential for their growth, development, and movement beyond the status quo.

CHAPTER 7

The Distinguished
Professor

*Yong sits at the kitchen table in a bright, cheerful home in East
Lansing, Michigan, in the winter of 1996. Penelope Peterson and
Patrick Dickson, who served on the search committee that hired
Yong, have invited him for breakfast. Over scrambled eggs, hash-
browns, toast, and coffee, the three discuss the annual meeting of
the American Educational Research Association. Penelope, AERA's
president, voices what she feels is the greatest challenge of the job:
organizing the annual meeting attended by more than 10,000
researchers and educators from around the world.*

*Penelope explains why she finds the task overwhelming: the
logistics of fielding thousands of proposals submitted for paper presentations, roundtables, poster sessions, and so on, for the annual
conference are daunting. As the proposals come in, they must be
read and assigned to reviewers whose expertise matches that of the
proposers. The proposals must then be transmitted to the appropri-
ate reviewers who must read and evaluate each and then complete
a form with their comments and recommendations. As each proposal is evaluated by at least two reviewers, someone must decide*

whether to accept or reject each one. Then, the decisions must be communicated to the proposers. Managing the process and recruiting the thousands of volunteer scholars needed to be reviewers is a formidable undertaking. The proposals come in USPS packages or express mail services and must be sent to reviewers, who then have to send them back to program chairs. Just the back-and-forth mailing costs a lot of anxiety, time, and money. The cost for some scholars submitting from other countries is discouraging. After the proposals are reviewed, successful ones must be organized into hundreds of different sessions, scheduled, and assigned meeting spaces that are typically spread across several hotels. Adding to Penelope's concerns, each year the number of proposals submitted grows significantly.

Listening to Penelope's frustrations, it occurs to Yong that digital technology can help solve this problem. Without a concrete plan in mind for how he will accomplish it, he announces to Penelope, "You know, I think we can do a lot of this online. We could create a platform for submissions."

Having never heard of such a thing, Penelope sits in startled silence.

Penelope's husband, Patrick, an educational technology expert, chimes in with great enthusiasm. "I think it is possible. It will require some resources, but it's doable."

After considering the idea for a moment, Penelope says, "We'll need a proposal that we can take to the board for approval. Can you put something together for the board meeting?"

Yong doesn't hesitate, saying, "I can have something to you in a couple of weeks."

The AERA board needs a few meetings to discuss the proposal, but they ultimately approve it as a pilot for the 1998 meeting for one of the larger subgroups (Learning and Instruction).

As the saying goes, be careful what you wish for. Once Yong gets the go-ahead from AERA, he and his team work feverishly

*around-the-clock for the next several months to meet the deadline.
He has little time for sleep between working on the project, teaching, writing articles from his dissertation, and collaborating on a
proposal for a major federal educational-technology grant. In addition, Yong helps his family settle into a new home and welcomes a
daughter, Athena, into the family. (In her honor, Yong names one
of the submission system computers Athena. To avoid favoritism, he
names another Tiger, his son's nickname.)*

*Remarkably, when the online portal opens for submission in July,
it works! A few bugs surface, but that is to be expected. Prior to the
AERA meeting in 1998, few know who Yong is. After that meeting,
his reputation takes off.*

In this chapter, we follow Yong as he takes a series of jobs to support his family after they join him in the United States. After a
position at Willamette University doesn't work out well, he lands a
job working on a joint project with Hamilton College and Colgate
University in New York. This enables him to further develop his
technology skills as he helps create a platform to allow course-sharing
between the two institutions at the same time he is completing his
dissertation. Expecting to earn his PhD soon, Yong applies for and
is offered a position as an assistant professor at MSU. After arriving
at MSU in the fall of 1996, he proposes and develops an online
proposal submission portal for the annual AERA meeting. He also
helps win federal funding for a project to create "computer clubhouses" in Michigan communities to increase student engagement,
collaboration, and online learning. He also continues to publish at
a prodigious rate and receives multiple opportunities to speak about
educational technology. He is asked to work on a language-learning
project between the U.S. Department of Education (ED) and the
Chinese Ministry of Education (MOE). Through these activities, his
reputation continues to grow, both nationally and internationally,

and his network of government officials, researchers, and educators expands. In recognition of his accomplishments, MSU awards Yong the title of University Distinguished Professor. Yong is the youngest professor to earn this recognition.

Temporary Jobs

In the summer of 1994, before his second year, Yong's life changed dramatically when his family joined him in the United States. When he picked them up at O'Hare Airport in Chicago in the rental car he had driven up from Urbana-Champaign, he was overjoyed to see them but disappointed that his son, Yechen, then just three years old, didn't recognize him at first. It had been over a year since he had seen his father—nearly half the boy's lifetime. On the return journey to Urbana-Champaign, Yechen repeatedly begged him to slow down. Accustomed to Chinese roads and drivers, he was frightened by the speed of the vehicles on the highway.

Yong now faced another challenge: how to support his family when neither he nor his wife were legally allowed to work outside the university. His visa did allow him to work as a teaching assistant but not outside of the school. In desperation, he took whatever jobs he could find. He got a job on campus serving breakfast at one of the student cafeterias. One day, he saw an ad on a bulletin board for delivery drivers for a local pizzeria. He convinced the owner to pay him under the table so neither of them would get into trouble. The owner had difficulty keeping drivers as the pay was low and the work often unpleasant and occasionally dangerous.

Yong was tasked with delivering pizzas in some of Urbana-Champaign's poorest neighborhoods, where crime rates were high. Customers were often irritated if the pizza was delivered later than they expected or arrived cold, even though this was not Yong's fault. Angry customers didn't tip him and even sometimes refused to pay for the pizza (in the days before online payments). To avoid irritating customers, he risked getting traffic tickets for speeding, which could also expose his visa status and might result in deportation. One night, exhausted from a day of serving breakfast early, completing intense research in the library, writing a required paper, and helping his wife make dinner and care for Yechen, he was rushing to deliver a pizza when another vehicle crashed into his aged Toyota Corolla. Shaken but only slightly injured, he took the accident as a message from the cosmos to quit the delivery gig.

In addition to the challenge of staying employed, Yong and Xi grappled with how to manage in a country that operated so differently from their home country. In socialist China, they'd owned virtually nothing. Most of what they needed to live was provided for free or at minimal cost. Chinese universities provided housing for faculty and for students. This included utilities, maintenance, and janitorial services. Meals in the university cafeterias were heavily subsidized and, therefore, very cheap. Universities and schools offered free bus service for students and employees. Public transportation was also cheap and ubiquitous. Basic healthcare was available for a minimal cost.

In the United States, Yong discovered that not only did he need to find an apartment and pay rent, but he also had to cover utilities and telephone service. Public transportation was limited, especially in smaller communities such as Urbana-Champaign. A car was necessary to travel to supermarkets and other places not accessible by public transportation. The initial outlay for a car was just the beginning. Additional expenses included insurance, fuel, maintenance, and campus parking. Seemingly, everything cost something and required understanding unfamiliar systems like car registration and emissions inspections. Managing the family budget on top of everything else was more than Yong could handle. When Xi arrived, Yong handed her his checkbook and said, "You are in charge of the money." Xi manages the family finances to this day.

Over time, the family adapted to life in the United States, and Yong's prospects improved. By 1995, Yong had earned his master's degree, and his committee approved his dissertation proposal. Now able to apply for academic jobs, he searched in earnest for a position that would allow him to support his family. He secured his first academic position in the United States with Willamette University in Oregon to lead their Language Learning Center.

That summer, he and Xi rented a Ryder truck, loaded up their family's few belongings, and headed west. They set up a small bed just behind the front seats so that Yechen could nap along the way. Although saddened to leave behind the friends he had made at UIUC, Yong was excited at the prospect of having a job that, despite the low pay, would enable him to support his family and continue to work in higher education. He was also excited to afford Xi and Yechen the opportunity to drive across the middle and western United States.

Shortly after they arrived in Salem, Oregon, and Yong began working in the Language Learning Center, he sensed a problem with his supervisor. For reasons Yong never fathomed, she seemed to take an immediate dislike to him. Given his accomplishments at UIUC and in China, she may have worried that Yong would take her job. Whatever the reason, nothing Yong did seemed to satisfy her. Although he enjoyed working with the students, the supervisor's animosity created an unpleasant atmosphere at the Center. Stressed already by the need to care for his family as they adjusted to a new environment and by the pressure to complete his dissertation, Yong began looking for a way out.

Software Development

In 1996, an opportunity arrived in the form of a job opening at Hamilton College in upstate New York that would allow Yong to develop his programming skills. With funding from the Mellon

Foundation, Hamilton was collaborating with nearby Colgate University to create a way for students at both institutions to take shared online language courses and receive credit at their home campus. A few universities offered online courses in the late 1980s and early 1990s, but universities had not yet begun collaborating to offer shared courses because of concerns about quality control and accreditation. Yong, however, immediately saw the potential of such a project.

Yong was excited at the prospect of building something new that fit his interests, tapped into his prior experience, and offered him the chance to learn new skills. In addition, Hamilton and Colgate reminded him of Linfield—a liberal arts college that focused on teaching and learning.

Yong traveled to New York to meet with the project leaders, and they were impressed by his skills and vision. After securing the job, Yong resigned from his position at Willamette, thankful and relieved to be free of the tense situation with his supervisor.

Yong and Xi once again packed up their few belongings. Rather than drive, they took the train, a three-day trip from Salem to Utica, New York, their new home. Uprooting the family so soon after arriving in Willamette had been trying, but Xi, like her husband, was always up for adventure. For Xi, the long train ride mirrored the cross-country drive that Yong had made with Keith three years earlier. Like Yong, she marveled at the landscapes she saw on the way to Chicago and then along the smaller of the Great Lakes. By the time they reached Utica, the Zhaos had seen more of the United States than most of its residents and much more than the typical international scholar.

The small town they now called home proved to be a good environment for the family. Hamilton provided housing in one of the vintage homes on campus. To Xi's joy, everything they needed was within walking distance. She and five-year-old Yechen enjoyed

roaming the leafy campus with its brick pathways and historic buildings. In the evenings, Yong made time to play with his son and catch
up with Xi. They enrolled Yechen in a kindergarten program, where
he made friends and improved his English. They bought a car, a
Saturn, and could finally afford to eat out and go to the movies.

In July, the family returned to Urbana-Champaign so Yong could
defend his dissertation. Relieved and gratified to have "PhD" added
to his résumé, Yong began the drive back to Utica. As he drove
and Xi and Yechen dozed off, he thought of his family in China.
Although his parents were unlikely to understand exactly what a
PhD was, they would no doubt understand that he had accomplished what very few others had. He took satisfaction in knowing
he was making them proud.

The small boy from Sichuan Province had come a long way. Yong's
lifelong trust in his instincts, hard work, and chance had created
possibilities that didn't exist for him as a boy. Opportunities had
appeared in his life, and he hadn't failed to pursue them, especially
those in the United States. At the same time, Yong knew that, as
comfortable as his family was becoming with life in their adopted
country, not everyone was comfortable with them.

In a small town in Indiana, the family stopped to eat at a Bob
Evans restaurant. As they waited to be served, Yong noticed the host-
ess seating customers who had arrived after him, blatantly ignoring
his family. Finally, Yong got up and approached a server and asked
to speak to the manager. He told the manager that he and his family
were clearly being discriminated against and that he intended to let
the central office know. Clearly distressed, the manager not only
ensured Yong and his family were served immediately, but he also
comped the meal. This was not the first or last time Yong would
encounter discrimination, but it was one of the most memorable,
perhaps because it was a reminder that whatever his successes and
accomplishments, others would judge him based on his appearance.

Although he appreciated many aspects of U.S. culture as well as its civil liberties, he recognized that racism, xenophobia, myopic nationalism, and bigotry lurked beneath the surface. Reflecting on the experience, Yong understood viscerally the analogy that Claude Steele used to communicate the phenomenon *stereotype threat* (that is, people of color's common experience of constantly being exposed to the threat of discrimination in a predominantly White world): you enter a house expecting to relax, only to learn a snake is on the loose. You never know when the serpent of bigotry will suddenly rear its menacing head.[127]

The family returned to life in Clinton, where in addition to developing the platform to enable Hamilton and Colgate students to take language courses online, Yong was creating a new piece of software called Homepage Maker. This software enabled faculty to craft their own homepages to house course materials and other documents and to facilitate asynchronous discussions. This was another example of software Yong designed that provided faculty with online tools that anticipated Blackboard (www.blackboard.com), Canvas (www.instructure.com), Moodle (https://moodle.org), and other course management platforms. Blackboard, the most widely used content management system, did not appear until a year later, in 1997.[128]

The work for the project helped him build on his already considerable software design and coding skills. Yet, he still did not consider himself a tech guy. For him, digital technology was the means to larger, more useful ends. Yong wanted to know, How do we enable students to access academic content more easily? How can we reduce the time faculty spend on administrative tasks so they can spend more time working with their students? Reaching these goals were, for Yong, learning exercises. This is what excited him. At the same time, he was no more prepared to tackle the challenge posed by the Mellon project than he had been to create the data analysis tool for the Chopsticks project or the HyperCard project at UIUC. He had yet to receive any formal training in software development. Ever the pragmatic adult learner, he learned precisely what he needed to know when he needed to accomplish his goals.

His work on the Mellon project and his articles and presentations about his work got him noticed. The Hamilton-Colgate project was one of three that Mellon was funding to demonstrate the feasibility of inter-institutional collaboration to provide shared online courses. At a conference on technology and language learning at Middlebury College in Middlebury, Vermont, Yong's presentation drew more interest than any other. Afterward, several attendees approached him with invitations to apply for positions at their institutions. Yong, however, was intent on a tenure-track position. He was ready—no more short-term projects.

To that end, he applied for an educational technology assistant professor position at MSU. The College of Education at MSU, under the leadership of Dean Carole Ames, was investing in educational technology and searching for early-career scholars who could help the college establish credibility in the field. Yong's two-day visit to MSU went well. His job talk was grounded in the work he had done at UIUC and the Chopsticks project. Because the dean was away during Yong's initial visit, he returned to East Lansing to meet her. When the job offer came shortly after this visit, Yong didn't even ask about the salary before he accepted. For people who had only just managed to scrape by all their lives, Yong and Xi were overjoyed at the College of Education's offer. Not only was the salary generous by Chinese standards (although average for new assistant professors at Big Ten institutions), but they also received medical care benefits and, to their great surprise, a moving expenses allowance.

The difficult part was having to tell the project leaders at Hamilton that he was leaving after only three months. They had been generous to him and his family, and he had enjoyed the project and the college. At the same time, they no doubt understood that Yong would be foolish to turn down a tenure-track position at a top research institution. For the third time in two years, Yong and Xi packed up their few belongings and set out on yet another adventure. This time, however, they believed they had found a place to settle down.

The Computer Clubhouse Project

When Yong joined the College of Education faculty at MSU in the fall of 1996, he hit the ground running. With his dissertation behind him, an H1 visa in hand, and his family settled first in East Lansing and then nearby Okemos, Yong was eager for a new project. The opportunity came in the form of a request for proposals from the U.S. Department of Education for funding through the 21st Century Community Learning Centers Program. The department had made educational technology a priority and hoped to spur innovation.

Yong worked with others, including Barbara Markle, to write a proposal that received $4 million in funding. The grant enabled the College of Education to collaborate with nine urban and rural districts that enrolled large numbers of students at risk. The project created ten after-school computer clubhouses in the collaborating districts. The goals included increasing student engagement in learning using computers and the web, offering authentic service-learning opportunities, promoting collaboration among students and their communities, and creating models of collaborative learning through shared resources.

The project took Yong to school districts all around Michigan. He worked with school personnel, students, and community leaders to tailor the clubhouses and activities to the local contexts. He hoped that students would become proficient in using digital technology and, in the process, become resources for their communities. In some of the rural districts he visited, he realized that he might be the first person of Asian heritage that local folks had met. To some, he was a curiosity, and to others, a suspicious foreigner. As had happened throughout his life, however, his easy manner, humor, and authenticity enabled him to work successfully with people whose backgrounds were dramatically different from his.

As they evolved, the computer clubhouses were not exactly what Yong had envisioned. He saw them as an opportunity for students to exercise their creativity and curiosity and to create products that would both serve their communities and demonstrate to themselves their capacity for innovation. In some cases, this did happen. For example, students took digital cameras from the clubhouse and documented the everyday lives of local people, to the delight of community members. Fishermen's wives laughed to see photos of their husbands at work on their boats, and parents smiled with pride seeing their offspring on the football field. A student created a website for a local bed and breakfast to advertise and book guests on the internet (decades before Airbnb).

Too often, though, adults intervened, and the products became more their design than the students'. Yong realized that most adults feel it is their responsibility to tell students what they should know or do and design projects for students to carry out. They underestimate the true capacities of students and create classroom contexts that reinforce their beliefs. Students are smart. They learn early in their school careers that when facing a problem or question, if they wait long enough, an obliging adult will solve the problem or answer the question for them. American students are experts at off-loading cognitive freight.

The original idea of the clubhouses had been to free students from the restrictions, expectations, and culture of the classroom so they could explore and create on their own. Unfortunately, in many cases, the local adults in the project superimposed the grammar of schooling on the clubhouses. Yong began to wonder whether schools as systems were, in a sense, irredeemable. Were the beliefs about learning—and learners and educators' roles—so hardwired that attempts at change were a lost cause?

With no immediate way to answer these questions, Yong turned his attention toward a new project. However, the questions remained planted in his subconscious, like dormant seeds just waiting for the right conditions to take root.

The AERA Submissions Platform

As the vignette at the beginning of this chapter chronicles, Yong's proposal for the online submission portal is yet another example of his faith in his capacity to do what others had not even imagined. To commit to delivering a product that neither he nor anyone else had previously envisioned was the kind of risky bet he had made before and would make again. He was betting on his ability to learn what he needed to know and to muster the information, skills, energy, and imagination required. He was not, of course, starting from scratch. He had significant experience beginning with the Chopsticks project and continuing through to the Mellon project.

Nonetheless, his promise to Penelope Peterson and the AERA board was highly risky. If he couldn't deliver in time or if the platform proved difficult to navigate for the technologically inept (of which there were many in academia in 1998), Penelope and the AERA would be in a fix. They would have to scramble at the last minute to ensure proposals were properly reviewed, submitters notified, and sessions scheduled. Because scholars from around the world depended on the AERA annual meeting both to disseminate the results of their research and to learn the latest from colleagues, any confusion or malfunction would be costly and embarrassing.

For Yong, this was another test. He was drawn to possibilities that others might shy away from because of the potential for failure, embarrassment, or losing face. He enjoyed testing himself with tasks that, on the surface, appeared daunting. Could he pull this off in the time available? Would this be the venture that proved too much for his skills and determination? Or would he rise to the occasion as he had done before? These unknowns drew him toward the flame; the uncertainty energized him.

Yong led a team of graduate students to develop the system. When the deadline for proposal submissions arrived, the platform was ready. Like any new system, users uncovered a few glitches. But these were rare, especially for what was essentially still a beta version of the platform. Yong and his team continued to manage and improve the system for the next five years. In addition to the development dimension of the project, Yong was also interested in researching it as a case study of the diffusion of technological innovations. Two of his doctoral students wrote their dissertations based on data from the AERA online submission platform.

Yong's success earned him greater recognition and more accolades. Through the process, he had rubbed elbows with many of the best-known educational scholars in the world, the power brokers (if we can apply the term to a field that has proved less than powerful) in educational research. The experience reinforced his understanding that he could converse on an equal footing with anyone regardless of their status, achievements, or reputation. Another quality he shared with his father: a self-assurance rooted in a well-earned high self-regard. Each time he took on a challenge and succeeded, his confidence in his abilities grew.

As with the Chopsticks project and language-teaching game, the Linfield experiences, the UIUC programs, and the Mellon project, Yong did not regard the AERA project as a stepping stone to something else. Rather, he saw it as an opportunity to learn, test himself, contribute to the field, and have fun. He had no clear idea what would come next. He did not set career goals and then calculate how to get there. No one knew what the future held. His goal was, and remained, to enjoy whatever is at hand and to look for and pursue opportunities that offered a chance to learn, grow, contribute, and enjoy himself.

International Connections

Another intriguing opportunity appeared in 2001 when the U.S. Department of Education and the Chinese Ministry of Education created a partnership and launched the development of prototype products to test the use of online technology for foreign language instruction. The original purpose of the U.S.-China E-Language Project, although not fully realized, was to create online lessons to teach the English language and U.S. culture to Chinese students, and Chinese language and culture to U.S. students.[129] The ED invited Yong to attend an early project-planning meeting in Beijing in September 2001, right after the 9/11 attacks.

Subsequently, Yong's proposal to develop the software as a game-based learning ecosystem was accepted by the ED. As the project unfolded, Yong became the primary advisor to the planning committee that met every six months. He worked closely with the software development team that the ED hired. The E-Language Project morphed over time, and when the ED focused resources elsewhere, the Hewlett Foundation stepped in and provided funding to Coastline Community College and the Learning Games Network that produced an online language-learning game, *The Forgotten World*.[130]

Through his involvement in this E-Language Project, Yong met high-level officials in both the Chinese MOE and the U.S. ED. His work on the project led to his involvement with the education group of the Asia-Pacific Economic Cooperation (APEC) organization. He was invited to accompany the U.S. delegation to multiple APEC meetings. The group consists of the education ministers of the twenty-one APEC nations who meet annually. In his opening remarks to the 2004 ministerial meeting in Santiago, Chile, the

Chilean Minister of Education Sergio Bitar praised Yong, who had been asked to speak to the group, as "brilliant."[131]

This is heady stuff for an associate professor (he was promoted and earned tenure after four years at MSU) who was not yet forty years old. For Yong, these international experiences reinforced his understanding that he had perspectives that both policymakers and scholars found valuable. His inherent disposition, reinforced by his experiences, to express his ideas candidly with no regard for conventions, paradigms, and orthodoxies made him a refreshing and provocative voice. Increasingly, he felt compelled to speak his truth to power. Policymakers and educators who were worried about the future and discouraged by the failure to improve student learning found his critique of the recent reforms provocative and thought-provoking.

In 2004, nineteen of the APEC ministers and other officials met in Beijing for the APEC Education Reform Summit. This meeting was Yong's idea. He helped organize it and secured funding from the Chinese MOE, the U.S. ED, the Chilean Ministry of Education, and the Sunwah Foundation. Yong saw value in the APEC participants learning from each other about educational reforms underway in the various countries. As each of the APEC members' education ministers spoke, describing the reforms taking place in their country, Yong was struck by the paradox that the speakers revealed: the Western countries represented at the summit reported that they were looking to the East Asian countries because of their success in mathematics and science on international assessments. For their part, East Asian countries described efforts to change their systems to more closely align with those of Western nations that they believed cultivated greater creativity and innovation. This paradox led him to begin rethinking many of his ideas, particularly about the capacity of educational systems to reform themselves, Western perceptions of Asian education, and the transferability of educational philosophies.

Big Questions

Yong's successes with grants, numerous publications, growing international prominence, and his students' high regard for his teaching and advising earned him full professor status in 2004. The following year, MSU named him a University Distinguished Professor. Yong was the youngest faculty member to receive this recognition, the highest honor the university bestows on faculty. He continued to reap outside funding for the College of Education. In 2005, he flew to Hong Kong to meet with a wealthy Chinese businessman and left with the promise of a $5 million donation to create the U.S.-China Center for Research on Educational Excellence. Unsurprisingly, the dean, Carole Ames, valued Yong very highly. But so did other deans around the country.

By the end of 2010, Yong was known throughout the educational world. He was no longer a rising star; he was a star. His accomplishments attracted the attention of deans and faculty at other prestigious institutions, including the University of Oregon (UO) in Eugene. Oregon had recently received a large donation from an anonymous donor who had made millions with Microsoft. The gift enabled the university president to create presidential chairs intended to lure star scholars to Eugene. The very first presidential chair was offered to Yong.

The Oregon offer created a dilemma for Yong. His family was comfortable and happy in Okemos. Both Yechen and his sister, Athena, liked their schools, and Xi had made friends and taken a job at MSU. But Yong had grown restless. Some of this stemmed from the evolution of his interests from educational technology-related issues to broader policy issues. Several factors contributed to this evolution, including his increasing involvement in international work and his realization that his greatest contribution might lie not in working for incremental changes in classrooms and schools but in tackling the big questions: What is education? Why do we educate our youth? Why has most of the world bought into an educational paradigm that may be harming students rather than helping them? What type of education will best prepare students for an uncertain future?

Moreover, he found that he was spending significant time on administrative work for the newly established Confucius Institute at MSU. He had been a primary force behind creating the institute and serving as the executive director but had not imagined how much administrative work it would continue to require. He longed for more time to devote to his scholarship. When the offer from the University of Oregon came, Yong knew he had to have a difficult conversation with his dean. Dean Carole Ames had supported and encouraged him and recognized and appreciated all that he had done for MSU's College of Education. She did all that she could to keep him there, but Yong realized he was ready to move on. The opportunity in Eugene was too attractive to resist. For one thing, it meant a return to a state he loved. Having spent time at Linfield and Willamette, he had come to appreciate the climate and the natural beauty of the Northwest. So, once again, he and his family packed up and headed west—to Eugene, Oregon.

Although happy to be back in Oregon, Yong encountered problems soon after he began his new job as associate dean of the college and the presidential chair. He found that, contrary to what he had been led to expect, his administrative responsibilities cut deeply into his time for research and writing. In addition, UO was enduring a period of upper-administration churn. During his six years at UO, Yong saw five presidents and five provosts come and go. In his own college, he worked with three different deans. This made for a lot of uncertainty and a lack of consistent direction. The job and the university were nothing like what he had imagined they would be.

Invitations to apply for other jobs kept coming, all of which he declined for five years. He kept hoping that the situation at UO would improve. However, by 2016, he was ready to leave. He was approached by Rick Ginsberg, the dean of the College of Education at the University of Kansas. Rick was a savvy veteran dean, adept at identifying and recruiting talent. The two began a conversation that eventually culminated in Yong becoming a foundation distinguished professor at the University of Kansas. Like the university distinguished professorships at MSU, the foundation distinguished professorship honor is reserved for a small, elite group of scholars.

These are not the only honors Yong has accumulated over the years. In 2003, the AERA awarded him the Raymond Cattell Early Career Award for Programmatic Research. He was elected to the International Academy of Education in 2005, at age forty, making him one of the youngest members of the organization. The Asia Education Foundation and the University of Melbourne, Australia, named him a Mangold Visiting Fellow in 2009. (Later, in 2020, he was appointed as a professor of leadership at the University of Melbourne.) In 2010, he received the National Leadership Award from the Institute for Educational Leadership. The magazine *Tech & Learning* included him among its list of the ten most influential people in educational technology in 2012. His book *World Class Learners: Educating Creative and Entrepreneurial Students* won the Judges' Award and the Distinguished Achievement Award from the Association of Educational Publishers in 2013.[132] The same book also won the Education Book Award from the Society of Professors of Education in 2013. In 2017, the Horace Mann League honored him with its Outstanding Public Educator Award. And in 2020, he was elected a member of the U.S. National Academy of Education. Not bad for a malnourished, barefoot kid who had failed as a sweet potato salesman.

To say that today he is among the best-known and most accomplished educational scholars in the world would not be an exaggeration. Yet, Yong himself is as surprised at what he has achieved as his friends back in Sichuan Province. There was no planning, no goal setting, and no expectations for what he would accomplish. He just followed his nose, saw opportunities, and jumped at them.

Cultural Identity

Over the course of Yong's life, he's been visited by vivid dreams that represent his unique and often conflicted identity as a traveler between cultures.

Yong is in the reading room of the UIUC library when the doors burst open and a herd of water buffalo file into the room, fanning out among the tables and bookshelves. Behind them stands Yong's father, holding a bamboo stick in his hand and calling out. Guang Ming's face wears an expression that Yong has often witnessed: he is watching the animals, but he is looking beyond the scene immediately in front of him. Yong feels a mix of emotions. He misses his father and the familiarity of herding buffalo. But he also feels a troubling sense of distance from the scene. It's like watching a film about a lost world, an irretrievable past. And suddenly, like a stone dropping into the pit of his stomach, he understands: there is no going back.

Yong has lived in two or more cultures most of his adult life. He has worked easily and successfully with people of different ethnicities, races, and faiths around the world. As a result, though, he has gone through emotionally challenging cultural experiences that, at the time, he didn't process. In addition to the buffalo-in-the-library dream, he's had several others that featured the theme of reconciling the two cultures in which he has lived most of his life. These seemed to express an underlying uncertainty about his cultural identity. This is likely a common experience for immigrants to any unfamiliar culture.

In one such dream, Yong is back in his home village. He watches as a large, Western-style ship filled with passengers trying to enter the village destroys the bridge spanning the nearby creek. The dream captures Yong's deep concern that his living in Western culture could bring disaster to his native culture. It captures his fear that the Westernized life he has chosen might be incompatible with his cultural roots.

In his final recurring dream, Yong returns to his village to participate in the annual Spring Festival celebration. People of different skin colors are scattered around the village enjoying a meal together. He's relieved and happy to see that a bridge is being constructed above the creek in front of his village. This dream, Yong realizes on waking, signifies a reconciliation for him between Western and rural Chinese cultures. After this dream, he is no longer visited by the conflicted dreams of his past.

These dreams occurred frequently across a span of twenty years. They did not trouble Yong so much as cause him to reflect on his identity and his relationship to the cultures in which he has lived and the world he has left behind. The disappearance of the dreams and the fading of his concerns about conflicting cultures underlined for him that the identity he has forged is not as a member of any single culture but as someone who is comfortable in any culture. He finds that the sobriquet *global citizen* best suits him.

Reflections

All the projects Yong worked on during this period have in common specific features: they were opportunities for Yong to learn, test himself, and create something new and valuable. Coming as he did from an obscure corner of the world with few possessions to his name, he had nothing to lose. What was the worst that could happen? He could fail. So what? He had started life with no material wealth, no social standing, no cultural capital, and no *guanxi*. Even if it all went to hell in a handbasket, the worst that could happen is he would return to square one. And he had proved to himself that even square one was not necessarily the end. Even square one offered opportunities if only, like his father, he stayed constantly on the lookout for them. Just as he had learned to swim by jumping into the village pond believing he'd figure out how to not drown *after* he got in the water, he jumped into projects with an unaccountable faith that he'd figure it out once he was on the inside.

With this mindset, Yong has an unusual approach to new possibilities. Risk aversion is said to inhibit people from taking on new projects and exploring new possibilities, which is true. But Yong never thinks about risks when taking on new projects. So, there is no "risk averse" because risk does not even cross his mind. He did not think about what would happen if he couldn't complete the project for AERA, the most influential organization in educational research in the world. He did not think about how little he knew the communities and the rural and inner-city schools in Michigan when he took on the Computer Clubhouse project. He never thought about the consequences of failure.

What drives Yong is the potential benefits of the projects and the excitement of learning new things. He enjoys the process of figuring things out. He compels himself to work out solutions to problems. He is innovative but also works very hard. In fact, he does not have any hobbies outside of work. To him, the work is so enjoyable that he does not need other things to distract or relax him.

Essential to Yong's successes, however, has been the support from institutions and colleagues. This observation may sound like a cliché, but it is true. Because Yong is not afraid to propose ambitious projects that often challenge the status quo and conventions, institutional leaders and colleagues might be hesitant to endorse his proposals. Yong was fortunate to be at MSU. Dean Carole Ames, Department Chair Richard Prawat, and other colleagues consistently provided him support. During her time as AERA president, Penelope Peterson also had faith in his project and made it possible. In fact, all his projects received generous institutional support.

But the kind of institutional support Yong has luckily experienced is not the norm, especially in traditional educational institutions. Schools tend to help children follow existing pathways that are already mapped-out roads to conventional ideas of success. As educators, we imagine that every student can work hard to travel along these prescribed pathways and reach their destination, which we hope is a happy life. In reality, the pathways that schools have students travel are grounded in evidence of the *past* instead of the possibilities of the future. Thus, when teachers encounter students whose ideas and pursuits do not fit the mandated curriculum and grade level, they are likely to provide less support to these outliers than to students whose ideas and interests are more conventional. In this age of state standards and high-stakes assessments, teachers are pressured to get as many students as possible to meet state expectations.

Everyone has a future, but all our futures are uncertain and unknown. The future for students, like that of everyone else, is shaped by the support they receive, the opportunities they encounter, their capacity to recognize and capitalize on these opportunities, and their desires to make a difference for themselves and others.

To help students discover or create opportunities, parents and educators should pay less attention to predefined pathways or the success stories of others. Cultivating the interests and capabilities of each individual student should outweigh mastering the required curriculum and staying on the conventional pathways. Instead, parents and educators should encourage students to explore new possibilities, search for opportunities to pursue whatever interests them, and risk failure. Such exploration, from a teacher perspective, is risky. From a student perspective, this is the way to learn about themselves, the world, and their interactions. This is how they learn about their interests and strengths, as well as how their interests and strengths can create value for others. More importantly, discovering, creating, and exploring new opportunities is itself learning. We cannot be prepared for new opportunities. Rather, we find opportunities and learn to explore and expand them.

CHAPTER 8

Themes in Yong's Thinking and Writing

Yong's improbable life led him to a wealth of experiences that uniquely placed him to engage with education's big questions. His ideas about these questions appear in his voluminous published works and multiple public presentations.

Rather than attempt to review even a representative sample of Yong's scholarship, in this chapter, we identify and summarize some of the key ideas and themes that run through his work. This is no small challenge as he has produced over 140 refereed articles and other professional publications as well as more than thirty books. In addition, Yong has published twelve articles in Chinese on educational technology; eighteen technical reports and commissioned papers; and twenty-five book reviews, conference papers, and other publications. Yong has also spoken at multiple events, including seventy-two refereed conferences, and has made hundreds of invited and keynote presentations. As a programmer, Yong developed fifteen software programs and web-based platforms. Thus, distilling his extensive body of scholarship down to a few key ideas is no small feat. In doing so, we recognize that we are likely doing a disservice to the breadth and depth of his work.

Problematic Educational Models

The book that best describes Yong's shift in thinking from insider to outsider is *Catching Up or Leading the Way*.[133] Written for the Association for Supervision and Curriculum Development (ASCD) and published in 2009, this book signaled Yong's gradual shift from an insider whose scholarship and activities focused largely on improving teaching and learning—especially using technology—to an outsider analyzing the prevailing narratives about both U.S. and Chinese education.[134]

The Chinese educational system is seen by some Western scholars and pundits as, if not a model of unvarnished success, a source of time-tested ideas to improve teaching and learning, particularly in mathematics.[135] They are dazzled by years of top-tier Programme for International Student Assessment (PISA) results and are engaged in a search for China's secret sauce. They tend to overlook factors that contribute to Chinese student success that include the sample of students who take the PISA and the system that is laser-focused on training students to be adept test-takers.[136] We wonder what the PISA scores would be if the sample included students from Western provinces such as Gansu, Yunnan, Henan, and Yong's home province, Sichuan. When China dropped a few spots in the PISA rankings, distraught Chinese officials hastily replaced Guangdong, which features a large immigrant population, with much more affluent Zhejiang. And, voilà! China was on top again.

This isn't to say that China lacks thoughtful, committed, and well-prepared educators. Nor is it to say that Chinese students, especially those in urban areas, lack knowledge, skills, and intelligence, especially when it comes to the high-stakes examinations they must master to work their way up the system, hoping to score high enough on the *gaokao* to land a coveted spot at one of the top universities. Rather, we argue that competition is fierce because the stakes are extremely high.

The system is not without its internal critics. China is paying the price for an educational system designed to produce compliant civil servants and employees. Families have become more vocally critical of a system that denies children, especially adolescents, their youth and opportunities to pursue interests other than academics.[137] At the same time, the CCP has recently moved to exert even tighter control over universities and schools under President Xi Jinping.[138]

Yet, like earlier reforms, this is another example of skirting the primary problem: an education system predicated on high-stakes examinations that privileges those with the resources to work the system. It is difficult to imagine how the system can be made more equitable and students' potential for independent and innovative thinking unleashed without fundamental changes in the examination gauntlet.

In *Catching Up or Leading the Way*, Yong provides evidence that, despite the perennial hand-wringing and teeth-gnashing over student scores on international assessments, the United States remained (at the time of publication) the most innovative country in the world.[139, 140, 141] China—the darling of PISA-obsessed scholars, thought leaders, and policymakers—was trying to transform its exam-driven system to foster greater creativity and innovation. In other words, it was trying to become more like the United States.

Factors that some critics pointed to as reasons that U.S. students failed to perform as well as Asian students Yong saw as providing the conditions for more creative thinking. That is, U.S. students spent less time in class, were assigned less homework, and engaged in more nonacademic activities such as music, art, and athletics. Less time in class or doing homework meant U.S. students had much more time for imagination and independent exploration of their environment. In the 1970s, researchers established an unsurprising link between time spent on an academic task and student learning as measured on standardized tests.[142] Given the significantly more time Chinese students spend studying, we would expect them to test better than their U.S. counterparts. Yong argued that the time U.S. students spend on nonacademic activities allows them more opportunities to explore and develop their interests, talents, and creativity.

In his next major book, *Who's Afraid of the Big Bad Dragon?* (to be known henceforth as the *Dragon* book), Yong digs even more deeply into the challenge China faces in promoting greater creativity and innovation and the reasons why the United States should not try to emulate the Chinese educational system.[143] He argues that a key to understanding Chinese culture as well as its educational system is the idea that Chinese society is horizontally competitive and vertically deferential. That is, Chinese compete with one another for grades, examination results, university places, jobs, the favor of their higher-ups, and so forth. At the same time, they are deferential and strictly accountable to the people above them in familial, institutional, organizational, and sociopolitical hierarchies. They are doggedly trying to surpass their peers while also currying favor with the higher-ups whenever possible. This isn't to say that all students are insincere in the respect they show their parents, teachers, professors, and others. Rather, the culture *demands* that they show deference even if they lack genuine respect for their higher-ups.

In education, this means that students constantly try to please their teachers and parents while diligently attempting to outperform their classmates. In an exam-based system such as that in China, to achieve these twin goals, they must excel on examinations. Many Chinese educators, parents, and officials are aware of this problem as well as the resulting decrease in student creativity and increase in student stress load. In recent years, officials have tinkered with policies in an effort (futile thus far) to significantly change the culture as well as the system. For instance, educational authorities have changed the exams, especially the *gaokao*, posing items intended to measure higher-order-thinking skills.[144]

Yet, anyone who has recently taught at a Chinese university will have noticed that students who matriculated in high school after the curricular and assessment reforms between 1990–2010 are still uncomfortable when asked to think independently. For instance, many struggle when asked to generate a question or topic for their own inquiry or research. This is true for graduate and undergraduate students alike. Many seem, at times, intellectually paralyzed by fear: any question they might raise is not sufficiently significant or original; they won't do well on their exams or thesis proposal; they will disappoint their families, teachers, and tutors; and they will not attain the careers expected of them.[145] Fear of failure leads them to avoid taking risks and to conceal what they don't know. If they believe they have failed to meet expectations, they have learned to blame themselves and readily take any failure or shortcoming as evidence that they are not sufficiently intelligent or diligent. Fear and self-doubt rarely breed creativity or risk taking.

Yong traces this risk-averse educational culture back to the highly competitive *keju* (imperial exam) system. The *keju* served to identify a select corps of scholars who had the intelligence and dispositions to help unify and stabilize the country for centuries but who, ultimately, impeded the economic and sociopolitical evolution China needed to join the Industrial Revolution. The focus on the Confucian classics in the *keju* diverted talented thinkers from studying mathematics and science and from the empirical mindsets that were critical to the development of an industrial economy. Moreover, Confucian values dictate absolute obedience to authority (parents, teachers, officials, and the emperor) as well as unquestioning acceptance of inherited knowledge. Finally, the *keju* system ensured that those most likely to cause or foment trouble (meaning the educated) would fill government positions that gave them a stake in maintaining the status quo. Yong's account of the *keju* system offers context for understanding the difficulties China faces in reforming an educational system ill-suited to producing innovative thinkers and doers.

Schooling as a Mechanism of State Control

The *Dragon* book also captures Yong's concern about the narrowness of Chinese students' learning experiences as well as a warning that U.S. educational policy seems to be headed toward similar constrictions. As in other countries, the Chinese government dictates the curriculum and approves textbooks. Private schools must also follow the state-mandated curriculum for grades 1–9, and middle school students must pass a state-mandated examination to graduate. Under General Secretary Xi Jinping, state control over the curriculum has tightened, and patriotism instruction has assumed greater prominence. International content and textbooks are banned in the compulsory grades (1–9), although international schools can use these sources in grades 10–12.[146] Rather than allowing schools the flexibility to better tailor the curriculum to their students, the Xi government has expanded its control, restricting student exposure to ideas and information from non-Chinese sources.

This type of monolithic control over the content that students study is precisely one of the reasons Yong believes that China, despite student success on PISA, is heading in the wrong direction. Yong saw a similar, although less authoritarian, trend toward standardizing and controlling content and assessment in the United States with the passing of the No Child Left Behind (NCLB) Act of 2001 and the Race to the Top Act of 2011.[147, 148] In fact, his concern was a primary reason he wrote the *Dragon* book. Underlying these landmark policies is U.S. policymakers' conviction that standardizing the curriculum and holding schools responsible for student standardized test results will produce better and more equitable results for students.

Yong argues that standardizing curriculum content, opportunities to learn, and learning goals flies in the face of what we know about human development and diversity. People differ in their abilities, dispositions, interests, and developmental trajectories. This fact lies at the core of Yong's educational philosophy. The corollary is that everyone should have the opportunity to discover and pursue their interests and abilities. Providing individuals with opportunities to develop their abilities and passions is in everyone's best interest. Controlling what, where, and how students learn diminishes their chances of discovering their interests and abilities as well as opportunities to develop them. While persuasive arguments for a common core of fundamental knowledge can be made, such a core can and should allow for expanded individualized opportunities to learn.[149]

Yong adopted the phrase *jagged profile of abilities and desires* to capture the fact that everyone has their unique set of strengths and weaknesses and different developmental schedules due to the interaction of their natural abilities and interests with their environment.[150] To realize their jagged profile, students need the time and freedom to explore, investigate, daydream, struggle, try and fail, and try and succeed on their own terms. The more students are constrained to prescribed curricula, inflexible schedules, and conventional learning spaces, the less time and opportunity they have to discover their abilities and passions.

Daydreaming or mind-wandering, while negatively associated with focused tasks such as reading comprehension, is also associated with autobiographical planning and creative problem solving.[151] Were students allowed more freedom and time to mind-wander, the fundamental law of probability dictates the next Srinivasa Ramanujan, Albert Einstein, Madame Curie, Rudolf Nureyev, Shirley Jackson, Yo-Yo Ma, Nas, Chu Bong-Foo, Shunpei Yamazaki, Steve Jobs, Rachel Carson, and Marcel Duchamp are more likely to emerge. Innovators such as these often discover their talents, passions, and creativity *outside* of formal educational settings. In fact, some, like Einstein, did just well enough to keep parents and teachers happy.

In school, Einstein apparently was frequently scolded for daydreaming.[152] Yet, he still managed to perform well enough to succeed in school and, on his second try, pass the entrance exam for the Zurich Polytechnic.

Yong's analysis of educational systems across the globe led him to understand that supporting students to develop their interests and abilities is not the primary purpose of these systems. Rather, for modern nation-states, educational systems serve largely to control the population, to focus their learning on the ideas and information that the leaders deem most valuable for the nation-state. National leaders do not hide this. Their rhetoric reveals that they see education as critical to a globally competitive economy. Chinese leaders who decry the failure of Chinese education to produce innovators do so because they see innovation as essential for China to continue to develop economically with the goal of international economic predominance. Similarly, U.S. leaders want education to prepare students to become globally competitive.

Yong views the United States as moving toward more constraints and less freedom for students. The movement of U.S. policy in the direction of standards, assessment, and accountability has been a shift toward greater central control of the curriculum. As he wrote in 2009:

> While the United States is moving toward more standardization and centralization, the Asian countries are working hard to allow more flexibility and autonomy at the local level. While the United States is investing resources to ensure that all students take the same courses and pass the same tests, the Asian countries are advocating for more individualization and attending to emotions, creativity, and other skills. While the United States is raising the stakes on testing, the Asian countries are exerting great efforts to reduce the power and pressure of testing.[153]

When an educational system prioritizes high-stakes assessments and enacts consequences for schools and districts that fail to meet predetermined criteria, educators focus disproportionately on the subjects that are tested (mathematics, science, and literacy) and slight those that aren't (the arts, music, history, and social studies):

> The reformers have chosen test scores in a limited number of subject areas (the core academics) over diversity, individual interests, creativity, and the risk-taking spirit that has helped sustain a strong economy and society in the United States.[154]

Moreover, these assessments ignore much of the knowledge and many of the skills and dispositions that may be of increasing importance as a very uncertain future unfolds.[155] That so many educators are becoming disheartened, retiring early, or leaving the profession entirely speaks to their frustration with the increased control that states exercise in their classrooms.[156]

Pernicious Effects of High-Stakes Assessment

A special target for Yong's concerns about the growing strictures on students' self-determined opportunities to learn is high-stakes assessments. In particular, he questions the value of PISA, which is administered by the Organisation for Economic Co-operation and Development (OECD). Chinese students (or a sample of five thousand Chinese students) typically come out on top of this triennial assessment of fifteen-year-olds. Global perceptions of Chinese education as a model for schools worldwide can be traced to this achievement. A primary rationale for PISA is to identify educational systems from which others can learn. The media, pundits, and think tanks helped to propagate the idea that the United States and other countries whose students perform well below those in China and other Asian countries need to emulate the star countries if they hope to improve their results.[157]

Technical and logical questions about PISA are numerous.[158] Yong questions specifically the validity of evaluating an entire educational system using data on the performance of five thousand fifteen-year-olds on a single test consisting of a limited selection of mathematics, scientific, and literacy items. This suggests that fifteen-year-olds around the world are comparable, that their cognitive abilities have developed similarly, and that they all have had similar opportunities to learn the specific content that PISA purports to assess. These appear to be unfounded assumptions. Moreover, this suggests that the content in these three curriculum areas trumps in importance any other content or skill set. Because teachers teach what is tested, prioritizing these three domains means other subjects are pushed to the margin or cut.

This largely ignores the importance of noncognitive skills such as socioemotional health, collaboration, critical thinking, communication, creativity, resilience, curiosity, self-regulation, and self-awareness. Researchers as well as several international organizations identify these skills and dispositions as being as important as (if not more important than) mastery of legacy school subjects for students' success, both in the present and for the future.[159] Acknowledging the limited domains of knowledge, skills, and dispositions that PISA claims to measure, OECD added, on an experimental basis, a simulation designed to gauge students' collaborative abilities.

A primary danger of PISA is how influential it is with policymakers and leaders around the world. Concerns about PISA rankings add fuel to the spread of neoliberal educational ideas globally. Neoliberal reforms typically include high-stakes assessments, curriculum standards, decentralization with school accountability, competition, and school choice—or what Andy Hargreaves and Dennis Shirley describe as *marketplace education ideology*.[160] Many countries use their PISA ranking to gauge the progress of their education reforms. The underlying assumption is that higher scores correlate with economic growth, a widely accepted claim that some researchers have challenged empirically.[161] In his INTED talk in 2020, Yong noted that although the United States ranked last on the First International Mathematics Study in 1964, the U.S. economy grew at an average annual rate of 3.3 percent while the average economic growth rate for the eleven countries with better test scores was 2.5 percent.[162] Yong advised his audience that if their economies weren't doing well, maybe they should just work to lower their test scores.

Personalized Education for All Students

Yong offers a counterview of education: rather than a one-size-fits-all, standardized experience, students need learning opportunities and resources tailored to their specific jagged profile. This does not obviate the need for students to learn a common body of knowledge and skills. All students deserve the opportunity to participate in the "great conversation," an opportunity that has been transformed by the internet. However, this core body of knowledge need not fill all the available learning space. Students need some of that space, maybe most of it, to explore and indulge in mind-wandering. Only in this way will they learn what in this world engages them.

Certainly, teachers have central roles in this scenario. As Yong sees it, teachers need to redefine their roles not as archivists and distributors of knowledge but as guides, resources, mentors, coaches, and nudges. He recognizes that for teachers to assume these new roles, the policy environment in which they work must change. This, in part, accounts for his opposition to the standards, high-stakes assessments, and accountability regime of the past few decades. As well as flooding the available learning space with prescribed content, these policies severely constrict educators' latitude to exercise their professional judgment to act in the best interests of all their students.

In his book *Reach for Greatness: Personalizable Education for All Children*, Yong lays out his ideas that digital technology and the

internet offer opportunities all students need to realize their potential.[163] He goes further in affirming his belief that every student has
the capacity for greatness. The role of formal education should be
to support students in identifying and developing their strengths. In
doing so, education creates the conditions students need to realize their
greatness and to bring that greatness to bear in the service of others.

In *Teaching Students to Become Self-Determined Learners*,[164] he offers
educators specific suggestions for how to help their students find
and pursue their interests. He describes the steps involved in teaching problem solving, decision making, goal setting, self-regulation,
and self-advocacy. These are the skills he believes are needed for students to become self-determined learners. Helping students develop
these skills requires teachers to embrace the roles of mentor and
guide rather than that of purveyors of state-mandated subject matter. The easy accessibility of information, ideas, and data via the
internet relieves teachers of the need to be the primary sources of
such knowledge.

Technology Is Not a Silver Bullet

Although Yong's early career involved projects and scholarship
focused on educational technology, he never considered himself
exclusively or even primarily an educational technologist. Early in
his time at MSU, one of his colleagues expressed surprise at Yong's
broad interest in teaching, learning, and policy. He thought of Yong,
as did others, as a technology guy. Over time, in fact, Yong had
become increasingly convinced that educational technology as it was
being used in schools was unlikely to significantly change the learning experience for most students. This was because of the combina-
tion of classroom culture, teachers' traditional roles, and the policy
context. As he wrote in *Never Send a Human to Do a Machine's
Job*, published in 2015, technology does have the potential to make
teachers' jobs easier and transform their role to guide and resource.[165]

As he wrote in a 2015 article published by the National Education Policy Center:

> There is no reason to have human teachers do things that machines do better or more effectively. There is no reason to have human teachers perform routine, mechanical, and boring tasks when technology can do it. After all, the reason to have technology is to extend, expand, and/or replace certain human functions.[166]

But this has not been achieved broadly. Technology also has the potential to shift students' role from consumers of other people's products to makers of their own products. However, the policy context that includes narrow learning standards and high-stakes assessments perverts the creative potential of technology. The myopic focus on raising test scores in a few subject-matter domains limits educators to seeing technology as another tool to achieve this end.

This limited view of technology means that students rarely have a chance to wield the true power of information and communication technology (ICT) in service of their learning and development. The internet offers a treasure trove of learning opportunities in the form of online classes from anywhere on the globe, interactions with peers and experts around the world, rich data sets, instructional videos, libraries and art collections, music and dance performances, animation, and so on. The list of possible resources seems almost endless and continues to grow hourly. Yet, teachers often confine students to using the specific technologies they themselves have been trained to use.

Yong's critique of how educational technology is used (or, rather, misused) in classrooms complements his call for more personalized learning opportunities. A shift in the understandings of parents, educators, and policymakers about the knowledge and skills of greatest value to students in an increasingly globalized and uncertain world would logically lead to a rethinking of the role of ICT in student learning.[167] Standing in the way is a policy context driven by a neoliberal conviction that state control of student learning is necessary to compete in the global marketplace.

The Necessity of Global Thinking

Yong's background and experience have convinced him that the only way to solve the existential threats that the world faces is through global understanding and collaboration.[168] This is an idea that finds its way into many of Yong's publications and speeches. Addressing climate change, climate-driven population migration, water shortages, dramatic wealth disparities, and other global threats requires people with the ability to understand others unlike themselves, to communicate and cooperate with people from different backgrounds, and to set aside narrow interests to focus on common problems and solutions. ICT offers possibilities for students to develop these capacities. Connecting with people from around the world and exchanging ideas and experiences can prepare students to be active and productive global citizens and impress on them their responsibility for addressing the common threats humankind faces.

Again, governments act to limit their citizens' access to information and ideas that may lead them to question official policies and actions. This presents a challenge to educators who must find ways to promote their students' understanding of the interdependence of the world and the need for global cooperation in contexts in which such actions are seen as unpatriotic and anti-government. U.S. conspiracy theorists profit from constantly invoking the sinister evils of what they term the "new world order." Despite these circumstances, teachers can still find ways to help students pursue their interests and passions. To be a humanist, as Yong is, is to have faith in the ability of humans, given the freedom to do so, to create and innovate in ways that improve and enrich their society and the lives of others.

In the 21st century, that society is global, and "others" includes everyone in the world.

Reflections

Yong's writings include many other ideas and themes, which the scope of this book doesn't allow us to examine here. However, five recurring themes dominate his writing:

1. Despite student success on international assessments, Chinese leaders continue to struggle to change an exam-driven educational system that stifles individual student interests and initiative. Deeply held sociocultural beliefs about education and knowledge and the sheer size and inertia of the educational system are obdurate obstacles to meaningful change. Recent reforms are unlikely to bring improvement as they return the focus to ideological indoctrination on a level unseen since Mao's times.[169]

2. The U.S. embrace of neoliberal educational policies has been spurred by misunderstanding education as simplistic content memorization. This is in part a result of mischaracterizations of education in China and other East Asian education systems. These policies have narrowed the curriculum, undercut teachers' professional judgment, and imposed high-stakes testing. In the wake of debilitating memory loss during the pandemic, many schools have doubled down on the standard curriculum with interventions such as "high-dosage" tutoring.[170] Rather than taking this unprecedented disruption of schooling as an opportunity to radically rethink all aspects of education, educators seem disposed to returning to the *status quo ante* despite the stress many are experiencing.[171]

3. Everyone has a jagged profile of interests, abilities, and
    dispositions and needs opportunities and resources to
    identify and develop their strengths rather than to be
    funneled into a one-size-fits-all education. As historian
    Geoffrey Lloyd observes in *Cognitive Variations: Reflections
    on the Unity and Diversity of the Human Mind*:

    > We are all aware of the amazing diversity of human
    > talents. Some people are superb musicians, others
    > not, some good navigators, others not, and so on
    > through the entire gamut of our intellectual and
    > artistic skills. Without such diversity, there would
    > be far less of the creativity that we naturally prize
    > and celebrate.[172]

    If schools were genuinely committed to recognizing and
    capitalizing on the strengths students bring with them,
    they would expand students' opportunities to explore, try
    out, and develop that at which they can excel.

4. Government policies globally over the past few decades,
    driven by narrow learning standards and a preoccupation
    with high-stakes assessments, have restricted students'
    opportunities to identify, explore, and pursue their
    interests. This has been done based on the unsubstantiated
    belief that the result will be greater international economic
    competitiveness. Rather than promulgating policies
    intended to improve students' test scores, governments
    intent on improving their productivity might need to shift
    the focus instead to 21st century skills and other non-
    cognitive skills.[173]

5. Educational systems have failed to exploit the educational
    richness of the internet and digital technologies that
    could provide students with access to global educational
    resources and learning opportunities. Despite the
    plethora of misinformation and wild conspiracies online,

the internet is a cornucopia of learning opportunities. Supervision is needed to protect students from potential harm, but schools should consider allowing students to use their smartphones and tablets not merely for research but to find the collaborations and opportunities to learn that will help them pursue their interests.[174]

Overestimating Yong's impact on educational thinking would be difficult. He has consistently questioned the status quo and conventional thinking when most have gone along with the orthodoxy of the day. That such a diversity of organizations has invited him to speak to them is a testament to both his international reputation and the resonance his ideas have with educators and policymakers around the globe.

These ideas resonated in particular with the coauthor of this book, Bill McDiarmid, who has his own story of improbable opportunities and swimming against the current—a story told in the epilogue.

The Luck of Meeting Smart People

By G. Williamson "Bill" McDiarmid

Writing about how genes, environment, and chance shaped Yong's improbable path has allowed me to see these forces at work in my own life. I count meeting Yong Zhao as a particularly remarkable bit of luck.

In this epilogue, I share how events in my life led to our unlikely collaboration.

A Chance Meeting

In 1996, I was hurrying along a hallway to teach a class in Erickson Hall at MSU. Coming toward me was a fresh-faced young man with Asian features in the company of one of my colleagues. I recalled that a candidate for a newly created position in educational technology was in the building and guessed this was he. I stopped to greet this visitor, who smiled, extended his hand, and introduced himself as Yong Zhao. I welcomed him to the college and excused myself as I didn't want to be late for class. Later, I attended his job talk and was impressed with the software he had created, although I didn't at the time recognize how extraordinary was his development of analytical software in China in the late 1980s. That summer, I left MSU to take a job as director of a social science research institute at the University of Alaska Anchorage.

I was vaguely aware of some of Yong's work at MSU through the news I received periodically from the College of Education. Educational technology was not a focus of my scholarship, although, in 1997, I collaborated with two Alaska Native educators to create the first website to house Alaska Native history and culture materials (Alaskool.org). I had little reason to pay attention to his work.

In 2007, I spent five weeks as a visiting scholar at Hebei Normal University in Shijiazhuang, an industrial city southwest of Beijing. Conversations with educators and students, especially those in my English-language teaching pedagogy course, piqued my interest in Chinese education. When I returned to the United States, journalists and policymakers were touting the superior results of the Confucian countries (Hong Kong, Korea, Singapore, Taiwan, and Japan) on the Trends in International Mathematics and Science Study (TIMSS) exam. After learning from my Hebei Normal students about their experiences preparing for the university entrance exam (*gaokao*) and their experience in Chinese schools and university, I discovered that students in other Asian countries had similar experiences.[175] None of my graduate-level students had ever worked in collaborative groups, and few had done anything other than memorize their textbooks. And all were or had been completely preoccupied with preparing for the *gaokao* to the exclusion of all else.

For example, during a holiday excursion with several families, the teenagers on our small bus described schedules that left them with (at most) five hours to sleep. When I asked them what they would do if they had any free time, they all responded, "Sleep." One of them lamented that her schedule left her with no time for her favorite pastime: playing the piano. A mother of one of the teenagers told me that she gave up her medical practice so she could support her son in preparing for the *gaokao*. The family had also moved from their spacious apartment to a much smaller place nearer to her son's high school so he would spend less time in transit and, thus, have more time to study. To me, this sounded bonkers. I felt badly for these young people who were forced to sacrifice their teenage years to prepare for an exam that would shape their future.

At this time, U.S. schools were six years into the No Child Left Behind policies that mandated greater standardization, a curricular focus on three subjects, school accountability, and high-stakes assessments. These policies seemed to move the United States closer to the Asian model of education that some U.S. thought leaders viewed as a positive trend. Those who knew Chinese education well, however, warned that the policies would constrict student learning opportunities and stifle creativity.

I shared these worries. In 2009, I read Yong's book, *Catching Up or Leading the Way: American Education in the Age of Globalization*. I found it ironic that Asian countries were searching for a way out of their exam-driven, high-pressure systems at the same time the United States was marching toward a standardized, high-stakes testing system. The irony was lost on the American pundits and policymakers who held up Chinese education as a model for the United States. As I watched the impact of the NCLB policies on schools, teachers, and students, I saw evidence of precisely the problems Yong had identified—in a nutshell, the growing constraints on students and teachers. Moreover, test scores during and after NCLB had not improved, nor was the gap between White and Black student scores narrowed.[176] By their own measure, the NCLB architects and fans had failed. Yet, with Race to the Top policies, the Obama administration charged ahead along virtually the same path.

Subsequently, I read more of Yong's work. I found that I agreed with many of his views. I continued to learn more about Chinese education and recent history during frequent visits to China and Chinese schools. Between 2010 and 2017, I visited more than two dozen universities and schools, talking with educators and students. After retiring in 2017, I spent two to three months a year (until the COVID-19 pandemic) in Shanghai, living in different neighborhoods and teaching graduate courses at East China Normal University (ECNU) in Shanghai. During the pandemic, I continued to teach my courses via Zoom. I also met Yong again; he held a position like mine at ECNU.

In 2019, I did a talk for the faculty of a large Greek bilingual school in Athens, Greece, where I had been a teacher in the 1970s. In the talk, I described how technology was transforming the world of work and argued that schools were not preparing students for this rapidly evolving world. Because I knew of Yong's interest in the topic, I sent him a video of the talk to get his reaction. He watched it, liked it, and we decided to use it as a basis for a book on educating for uncertainty.[177]

As we completed that book, we discussed other possible projects. Yong had a contract to write an autobiography and asked if I wanted to collaborate on the book. I immediately agreed. For the next fourteen months, we met on Zoom every week. I interviewed Yong and recorded his responses via Zoom transcripts, which, along with some autobiographical stories Yong had previously written, constituted the primary sources for this book.

The project appealed to my sense of deep curiosity about people from different cultures. I find people's stories fascinating. In my life, I have sought to meet and get to know people who were culturally different from me, whose stories I wanted to hear, and from whom I believed I could learn. This was behind my extended visits to Sri Lanka, Pakistan, East Africa, Greece, and Alaska. So, when he suggested we work on the autobiography project together, I immediately agreed.

Southern Roots

My curiosity about people began in my childhood. I remember being told as a child that I was too curious, that I asked too many questions. I was interested in a lot of things, especially people, their stories, how and what they thought, and why. One of the few periodicals that came into our house was *National Geographic*. I skimmed each issue and spent hours tracing on onionskin paper the intricate maps tucked into each issue. I dreamed of someday visiting the places on these maps.

Growing up in the Jim Crow South of the 1950s and 1960s, I often found the world around me confusing. As a small child, I played with the sharecropper children whose families lived on my grandfather's and uncle's farm. I was confused when I was told I could not invite them into my grandfather's house. Nor was I allowed to visit their houses that were little more than shacks. When we went to the Saturday morning movies, I wondered why all the Black children had to climb rickety outdoor stairs to the balcony. On Sundays, we went to the all-White church in town, while the sharecropper families attended the immaculately maintained, small brick church built on land my grandfather had provided on the edge of the farm. Somehow, I knew not to ask the adults questions about this. When I was a preteen, I watched on TV as burly White men firehosed Black children and sent their German shepherds to attack them. Watching this was terrifying. Some of those being brutalized were my age. This didn't square with the lessons I was taught in Sunday school. If Jesus taught us that we should love everyone, how could Christians viciously attack children who were peacefully protesting?

By an extraordinary stroke of luck, a political science PhD student taught a summer school U.S. government course that I took to avoid taking the course at my high school, where the government teacher was notoriously boring and mean. A prime topic in the class was U.S. labor history, a subject very unlikely to be on the menu in southern high schools. In my research, I learned about the violence perpetrated against labor organizers and strikers with the connivance of the police. We also studied the *Brown v. Board* decision and the continuing resistance to integration. (An irony is that the course was taught in a *segregation academy* established for families who didn't want their children attending school with Black children.) Most importantly, I learned to be skeptical of what I was being taught— and increasingly aware of what I was not being taught—in school.

The graduate student invited me and a classmate to his house for conversations about history and politics. It was like a seminar and unlike any prior learning experience. When I went to college (my other option was Vietnam), I took courses in political science and history as well as literature and philosophy. A course on Reconstruction after the Civil War flipped the narrative I had been taught in high school on its head. As I read the work of scholars like John Hope Franklin, C. Vann Woodward, and Edmund Wilson, I understood how bogus the "lost cause" narrative about the Confederacy was that I had been fed not just by my textbooks but by the southern culture in which I had been raised.

My roots are in rural North Carolina. I was born on my grandfather's tobacco farm. My World War II veteran father failed at business, took advantage of the G.I. Bill to earn a college degree, and went to work as an administrator for various southern public health departments. My remarkably insightful mother was dyslexic (not a diagnosed condition in the 1930s) and was, reputedly, "gifted" her high school diploma. She secretly married my father the year before she graduated and raised six children over the next thirty years.

My father's job meant we moved frequently. We weren't poor; we always had adequate food and clothes. Because of the number of mouths to feed, we lived in neighborhoods that were working class or lower-middle class and attended local schools. After I entered high school, a large county comprehensive, my father's promotion enabled the family to move up to solid middle-class status.

Uncommon Interests

I was a B student, doing well in history and English, mediocre in science, and poorly in mathematics. My friends were mostly jocks, as was I. Beginning at age fourteen, I always had at least one weekend and summer vacation job. For eight years, I worked every summer and vacation for the same residential construction company. On weekend evenings, I flipped burgers and made milkshakes.

Although I participated in sports and other activities, high school didn't engage me intellectually. On my own, I read voraciously, mostly novels, history (especially about the Civil War), poetry, and biographies. I stumbled upon Sigmund Freud's *The Interpretation of Dreams* and became engrossed in understanding the unconscious and the role it plays in our behaviors.[178] None of my friends shared my interests. When the time came, I chose a university in another state. I wanted to experience a place and people that I didn't know, and I wanted to nurture my emerging identity as an intellectual.

I didn't know that I was an intellectual (or aspired to be) until one of my professors defined the term as "someone for whom ideas are both work and play." Bingo! There I am. I did not grow up among people who were interested in ideas, however intelligent they were in other ways. In fact, well-educated people were, in my context, frequent targets of ridicule. When I started university, my work-mates in construction mocked me incessantly, nicknaming me "the professor," and were hyper-vigilant for any sign that might suggest I thought I was somehow better than they were. Even some of my cousins teased me for going to an elite (public) university. When I read Richard Hofstadter's *Anti-Intellectualism in American Life*, I better understood the cultural and historical roots of the disdain that many in the United States show toward the well-educated.[179]

The myth of the fearless frontiersman succeeding in a hostile environment because of his practical skills and savvy continues to pervade U.S. culture. Manly men don't read books. They do manual labor, drink beer, and amuse their friends with racist and misogynistic jokes.

Opportunists

During my early visits to China, I came to admire the respect that scholars are accorded. Seeing statues of renowned scholars from China's past, I realized I had never seen a statue of a scholar in a public space in the United States, although I imagine a few may exist. If my Chinese students saw me on campus, they rushed to carry my backpack, open doors for me, add hot water to my tea thermos. Only after reading Yong's book, *Who's Afraid of the Big Bad Dragon?*, and discussing the Confucian tradition with him did I come to a more nuanced understanding of this tradition and its negative consequences.

As I got to know Yong through our collaboration, I realized that, despite the radical differences in the conditions we experienced as children and students, we shared certain experiences, personality traits, and outlooks. We both grew up among rural people who had little or no interest in ideas. Consequently, we both had inner lives where we played with ideas. Both of us were persistently curious, and our curiosity extended broadly to our environments, people, ideas, books, history, philosophy, and psychology, to name a few.

We both had, throughout our lives, jumped at opportunities based on hunches rather than considered thinking. In fact, we agreed that neither of us had a plan for our lives. (As a child, I wanted to be a professional baseball player until I understood the level of talent needed.) We had not set career goals or created future plans. Rather, we had looked for opportunities that afforded us the chance to learn, test our mettle and capabilities, and expand our horizons.

We also shared an acute awareness of the socioeconomic inequities that pervade the world. During college, through a series of chance events, I served as a public health volunteer on the HOPE ship docked in Colombo, Ceylon (now Sri Lanka) for a summer. This exposed me to the dire conditions in which many people in poorer countries live. I had seen crushing poverty in the lives of the share-cropper families on my grandfather's farm, but the poverty I saw in the streets of Colombo and in rural villages in Ceylon was at another level. I also saw resilient people in both settings working to address the wretched conditions in which many lived.

Later in my life, my elderly Morris Minor broke down in Athens, Greece, as I was driving to the Gulf of Aqaba in the Sinai, where a job awaited. I had no money but found a series of jobs and, in the end, spent more than seven years in Greece. Athens was a strategic jumping-off point for Europe, Egypt, East Africa, and the Middle East. In the 1970s, travel was more affordable if you were willing to use local transportation and live like the locals.

Among the many real-life adventure books I read as a teenager was Laurens van der Post's *The Lost World of the Kalahari*.[180] With some friends, I crossed the Kalahari in a vintage Land Rover and met a group of Kung. I explored the wetlands around Maun in Botswana by canoe and walked the backstreets of Mombasa in Kenya. Hitchhiking allowed me to spend time with locals as well as save money. In Cairo, my cheap hotel turned out to be a brothel where the helpful sex workers had a vast network of taxi drivers, shop owners, and street vendors. I got to know a Cairo that few Westerners experience, and I did it on the cheap.

Later, while in graduate school in Boston, I chanced upon a job ad posted on a bulletin board. It was for a research assistant for a scholar in a social science research institute at the University of Alaska Fairbanks. Speaking of luck, the bulletin board was in a building I only wandered into to avoid the rain. I mailed in my application and, to my surprise, got a letter back offering me the job. I loaded my few possessions (mostly books) into a secondhand pickup truck and drove across Canada and up the Alaska Highway to Fairbanks. For the next few years, I worked on research projects in rural Native villages and took a year off to teach in a tribal-run school in a village of 420 Cup'ik Natives on the Bering Sea. At that time, most families in the village survived through subsistence activities and lived without plumbing in little more than plywood shacks. Not much different from those of the sharecroppers.

Later in my life, I seized on other opportunities that my instincts told me could be chances to learn. For example, I got involved in a project with the Ismaili community in Pakistan that led to the creation of an educational research institute at the Aga Khan University in Karachi. As noted, I took advantage of opportunities to travel and teach in China. As a faculty member at five different universities, I created or renewed teacher preparation programs designed in collaboration with preK–12 educators and arts and sciences departments. I collaborated with colleagues in arts and sciences, computer science, and business to create a first-of-its-kind master's degree program in educational innovation, technology, and entrepreneurship. I viewed each of these initiatives as learning opportunities.

In the end, this is perhaps what Yong and I share most closely: the drive to learn, to understand the world and the people in it better, and to use this knowledge, we hope, to leave this world a better place than we found it. I am grateful to Yong for giving me yet another opportunity to learn.

Notes

Preface

1   Duffy, R. D., & Dik, B. J. (2009). Beyond the self: External influences in the career development process. *The Career Development Quarterly, 58*(1), 29–43. https://doi.org/10.1002/j.2161-0045.2009 .tb00171.x

2   Robson, K. L. (2005). Human, social, and cultural capital: Expressions of social position and determinants of life chances. Available from Sociological Abstracts. (60031044; 200602674).

3   Social Programs That Work. (n.d.). *Prenatal/early childhood.* Accessed at https://evidencebasedprograms.org/policy_area /prenatal-earlychildhood/ on June 24, 2022.

4   Chmielewski, A. K. (2019). The global increase in the socioeconomic achievement gap, 1964 to 2015. *American Sociological Review, 84*(3), 517–544.

5   Chmielewski, A. K. (2019). The global increase in the socioeconomic achievement gap, 1964 to 2015. *American Sociological Review, 84*(3), 517–544, p. 537.

6   Power, C. (2015). *The power of education: Education for all, development, globalisation and UNESCO.* Singapore: Springer. https://doi.org/10.1007/978-981-287-221-0

7   Britannica. (n.d.). *Great Leap Forward.* Accessed at www.britannica .com/event/Great-Leap-Forward on March 25, 2022.

8   Britannica. (n.d.). *Great Leap Forward.* Accessed at www.britannica .com/event/Great-Leap-Forward on March 25, 2022.

9   Britannica. (n.d.). *A brief overview of China's Cultural Revolution.* Accessed at www.britannica.com/story/chinas-cultural-revolution on March 21, 2022.

10   Phillips, T. (2016, May 10). The Cultural Revolution: All you need to know about China's political convulsion. *The Guardian.* Accessed at www.theguardian.com/world/2016/may/11/the-cultural-revolution -50-years-on-all-you-need-to-know-about-chinas-political -convulsion on March 21, 2022.

11   Britannica. (n.d.). *A brief overview of China's Cultural Revolution.* Accessed at www.britannica.com/story/chinas-cultural-revolution on March 21, 2022.

12   McDiarmid, G. W., & Zhao, Y. (2022). *Learning for uncertainty: Teaching students how to thrive in a rapidly evolving world.* New York: Routledge.

Introduction

13   Pluchino, A., Biondo, A. E., & Rapisarda, A. (2018). Talent versus luck: The role of randomness in success and failure. *Advances in Complex Systems, 21*(3.4). https://doi.org/10.1142 /S0219525918500145

14   Pluchino, A., Biondo, A. E., & Rapisarda, A. (2018). Talent versus luck: The role of randomness in success and failure. *Advances in Complex Systems, 21*(3.4). https://doi.org/10.1142 /S0219525918500145

15   Lewontin, R. (2000). *The triple helix: Gene, organism, and environment.* Cambridge, MA: Harvard University Press.

16   Lewontin, R. (2000). *The triple helix: Gene, organism, and environment.* Cambridge, MA: Harvard University Press.

17   Fea, J. (2020). *What is historical contingency?* Accessed at https:// currentpub.com/2020/08/18/what-is-historical-contingency on March 1, 2022.

18   Fea, J. (2020). *What is historical contingency?* Accessed at https:// currentpub.com/2020/08/18/what-is-historical-contingency on March 1, 2022.

19   Fea, J. (2020). *What is historical contingency?* Accessed at https:// currentpub.com/2020/08/18/what-is-historical-contingency on March 1, 2022.

20   Pluchino, A., Biondo, A. E., & Rapisarda, A. (2018). Talent versus luck: The role of randomness in success and failure. *Advances in Complex Systems*, *21*(03n04).

21   George, N. M., Parida, V., Lahti, T., & Wincent, J. (2016). A systematic literature review of entrepreneurial opportunity recognition: Insights on influencing factors. *International Entrepreneurship and Management Journal*, *12*(2), 309–350. https://doi.org/10.1007/s11365-014-0347-y

22   Baron, R. A. (2006). Opportunity recognition as pattern recognition: How entrepreneurs "connect the dots" to identify new business opportunities. *Academy of Management Perspectives*, *20*(1), 104–119.

23   Heinonen, J., Hytti, U., & Stenholm, P. (2011). The role of creativity in opportunity search and business idea creation. *Education + Training*, *53*(8/9), 659–672. https://doi.org/10.1108/00400911111185008

24   Shane, S., Nicolaou, N., Cherkas, L., & Spector, T. D. (2010). Do openness to experience and recognizing opportunities have the same genetic source? *Human Resource Management*, *49*(2), 291–303. https://doi.org/10.1002/hrm.20343

25   Shane, S., Nicolaou, N., Cherkas, L., & Spector, T. D. (2010). Do openness to experience and recognizing opportunities have the same genetic source? *Human Resource Management*, *49*(2), 291–303, p. 299. https://doi.org/10.1002/hrm.20343

26   Wiseman, R. (2003). *The luck factor.* New York: Miramax.

27   Soto, C. J. (2018). Big five personality traits. In M. H. Bornstein (Ed.), *The SAGE encyclopedia of lifespan human development* (pp. 240–241). Thousand Oaks, CA: SAGE.

28   Wiseman, R. (2003). *The luck factor.* New York: Miramax, p. 43.

29   Jauk, E., Benedek, M., Dunst, B., & Neubauer, A. C. (2013). The relationship between intelligence and creativity: New support for the threshold hypothesis by means of empirical breakpoint detection. *Intelligence*, *41*(4), 212–221. https://doi.org/10.1016/j.intell.2013.03.003

30   Lewontin, R. (2000). *The triple helix: Gene, organism, and environment.* Cambridge, MA: Harvard University Press, p. 38.

Chapter 1

31   Vermeer, E. B., Pieke, F. N., & Chong, W. L. (Eds.). (1998).
      *Cooperative and collective in China's rural development: Between state
      and private interests.* New York: Routledge.

32   The World Bank. (1978). *World development report.* Accessed
      at https://openknowledge.worldbank.org/bitstream/handle/10986
      /5961/WDR%201978%20-%20English.pdf on March 3, 2022.

33   Dikötter, F. (2010). *Mao's great famine: The history of China's most
      devasting catastrophe, 1958–1962.* New York: Walker.

34   Song, S. (2014). Malnutrition, sex ratio, and selection. *Human
      Nature, 25,* 580–595. https://doi.org/10.1007/s12110-014-9208-1

35   New World Encyclopedia. (n.d.). *Chinese calendar.* Accessed at
      www.newworldencyclopedia.org/entry/Chinese_calendar on
      April 5, 2022.

36   Asia Farming. (2019). *Sweet potato cultivation information guide.*
      Accessed at www.asiafarming.com/sweet-potato-cultivation on
      March 2, 2022.

37   Radio and television gradually replaced the ubiquitous loudspeakers
      in many villages. Under Xi Jinping, they appear to be making
      a comeback, blasting Xi's words of wisdom rather than Mao's.
      Loudspeakers have reportedly been recently installed in 10,000
      villages in Anhui Province. Gan, N. (2021). *Chinese people ordered to
      think like Xi as Communist Party aims to tighten control.* Accessed at
      www.msn.com/en-us/news/world/chinese-people-ordered-to-think
      -like-xi-as-communist-party-aims-to-tighten-control/ar-AAMdh2A
      on March 3, 2022.

38   McKenzie, K. (2019). The effects of poverty on academic
      achievement. *BU Journal of Graduate Studies in Education, 11*(2).
      Accessed at https://files.eric.ed.gov/fulltext/EJ1230212.pdf on April
      29, 2022.

39   Wagmiller, R. L., & Adelman, R. M. (2009). *Childhood and
      intergenerational poverty: The long-term consequences of growing up
      poor.* New York: National Center for Children in Poverty. Accessed
      at www.nccp.org/wp-content/uploads/2020/05/text_909.pdf on April
      29, 2022.

40   McCray, C. (2022). *Equitable instruction, empowered students: A teacher's guide to inclusive and culturally competent classrooms*. Bloomington, IN: Solution Tree Press, p. 5.

41   Murayama, K., Pekrun, R., Suzuki, M., Marsh, H., & Lichtenfeld, S. (2016). Don't aim too high for your kids: Parental overaspiration undermines students' learning in mathematics. *Journal of Personality and Social Psychology, 111*(5), 766–779.

42   Khattab, N., Madeeha, M., Samara, M., Modood, T., & Barham, A. (2022). Do educational aspirations and expectations matter in improving school achievement? *Social Psychology of Education, 25*, 33–53. https://doi.org/10.1007/s11218-021-09670-7

43   Khattab, N., Madeeha, M., Samara, M., Modood, T., & Barham, A. (2022). Do educational aspirations and expectations matter in improving school achievement? *Social Psychology of Education, 25*, 33–53. https://doi.org/10.1007/s11218-021-09670-7

44   Wang, S., Rubie-Davies, C. M., & Meissel, K. (2018). A systematic review of the teacher expectation literature over the past 30 years. *Educational Research and Evaluation, 24*(3–5), 124–179. https://doi.org/10.1080/13803611.2018.1548798

45   Xin Ma found that parents' expectations for their children's academic performance had a greater impact on performance than the expectations of their teachers. Ma, X. (2001). Participation in advanced mathematics: Do expectation and influence of students, peers, teachers, and parents matter? *Contemporary Educational Psychology, 26*(1), 132–146.

46   Mason, C., Rivers Murphy, M. M., & Jackson, Y. (2020). *Mindful school communities: The five Cs of nurturing heart centered learning*. Bloomington, IN: Solution Tree Press, p. 135.

Chapter 2

47   Zhao, Y. (2014). *Who's afraid of the big bad dragon?* San Francisco: Jossey-Bass.

48   Britannica. (n.d.). *The Sino-Soviet split*. Accessed at www.britannica .com/topic/20th-century-international-relations-2085155/The-Sino -Soviet-split on March 29, 2022.

49   Thøgersen, S. (2002). *A county of culture: Twentieth-century China seen from the village schools of Zouping, Shandong.* Ann Arbor, MI: University of Michigan Press.

50   Thøgersen, S. (2002). *A county of culture: Twentieth-century China seen from the village schools of Zouping, Shandong.* Ann Arbor, MI: University of Michigan Press, p. 7.

51   Thøgersen, S. (2002). *A county of culture: Twentieth-century China seen from the village schools of Zouping, Shandong.* Ann Arbor, MI: University of Michigan Press, p. 89.

52   Han, D. (2008). *The unknown Cultural Revolution: Life and change in a Chinese village.* New York: Monthly Review Press.

53   Pepper, S. (1987). New directions in education. In R. MacFarquhar & J. Fairbank (Eds.), *The Cambridge history of China* (pp. 398–431). Cambridge, UK: Cambridge University Press, p. 401. https://doi .org/10.1017/CHOL9780521243360.010

54   Milton, D. (1972). China's long march to universal education. *The Urban Review, 5*(5), 3–9. https://doi.org/10.1007/BF02333115

55   Milton, D. (1972). China's long march to universal education. *The Urban Review, 5*(5), 3–9. https://doi.org/10.1007/BF02333115

56   Milton, D. (1972). China's long march to universal education. *The Urban Review, 5*(5), 3–9, p. 8. https://doi.org/10.1007/BF02333115

57   Guo, G. (2007). Persistent inequalities in funding for rural schooling in contemporary China. *Asian Survey, 47*(2), 213–230. https://doi. org/10.1525/as.2007.47.2.213

58   This practice continues. Even university classes have monitors.

59   Deng Xiaoping reinstated the exam in 1977 as part of the post–Cultural Revolution educational reforms.

60   Wang, L., & Lewin, K. (2016). *Two decades of basic education in rural China.* Singapore: Springer.

61   Singer, M. (1971). *Educated youth and the Cultural Revolution in China.* Ann Arbor, MI: University of Michigan.

62   Singer, M. (1971). *Educated youth and the Cultural Revolution in China.* Ann Arbor, MI: University of Michigan, p. 83.

63　The death of Mao Zedong and the defeat of the radical Gang of Four brought Deng Xiaoping to power in 1977. Among the first changes Deng made in educational policy was to re-establish the examination system including the *gaokao* required for university entry.

64　Han, D. (2008). *The unknown Cultural Revolution: Life and change in a Chinese village.* New York: Monthly Review Press.

65　Han, D. (2008). *The unknown Cultural Revolution: Life and change in a Chinese village.* New York: Monthly Review Press. Many teachers also received a monthly stipend of two *yuan* from the commune government.

66　Shao, X. (2020). *The broken cart: A rural girl's journey through China's Cultural Revolution and beyond.* Author, p. 95.

67　This prejudice is pervasive, and not confined to China. Bill found a similar prejudice in the Greek high school in which he taught in the 1970s. The most prestigious and selective university in Greece at the time was the Polytechnic.

68　Shao, X. (2020). *The broken cart: A rural girl's journey through China's Cultural Revolution and beyond.* Author.

69　Shao, X. (2020). *The broken cart: A rural girl's journey through China's Cultural Revolution and beyond.* Author, p. 116.

70　Shao, X. (2020). *The broken cart: A rural girl's journey through China's Cultural Revolution and beyond.* Author.

71　Barr, R. D., & Gibson, E. L. (2013). *Building a culture of hope: Enriching schools with optimism and opportunity.* Bloomington, IN: Solution Tree Press, p. 73.

Chapter 3

72　Britannica. (n.d.). *Yellow River.* Accessed at www.britannica.com /place/Yellow-River on April 6, 2022.

73　Chen, Y., Syvitski, J. P. M., Gao, S., Overeem, I., & Kettner, A. J. (2012). Socio-economic impacts on flooding: A 4000-year history of the Yellow River, China. *Ambio, 41*(7), 682–698. See also: Normile, D. (2016, August 4). *Massive flood may have led to China's earliest empire.* Accessed at www.science.org/content/article/massive -flood-may-have-led-chinas-earliest-empire on September 9, 2022.

74   Cartwright, M. (2017, July 25). Mandate of Heaven. *World History Encyclopedia*. Accessed at www.worldhistory.org/Mandate_of _Heaven/ on April 6, 2022.

75   These tragedies convinced officials in the newly created PRC to invest heavily in flood-control projects, including the Three Gorges Dam on the Yangtze River.

76   Sichuan International Studies University. (n.d.). *About SISU.* Accessed at http://en.sisu.edu.cn/About_SISU.htm on March 3, 2022.

77   Sichuan International Studies University. (n.d.). *Facts and figures.* Accessed at en.sisu.edu.cn/About_SISU/Facts_and_Figures.htm on March 3, 2022.

78   Vogel, E. F. (2011). *Deng Xiaoping and the transformation of China.* Cambridge, MA: Harvard University Press, p. 207.

79   Rock, M. Y. (n.d.). *Background on the People's Republic of China (PRC).* Accessed at www.e-education.psu.edu/geog128/node/703 on April 6, 2022.

80   Jersild, A. (2014). *The Sino-Soviet alliance: An international history.* Chapel Hill, NC: University of North Carolina Press.

81   Reuters. (2008, May 19). *TIMELINE: Russia-China relations.* Accessed at www.reuters.com/article/us-russia-medvedev-foreign -timeline/timeline-russia-china-relations-idUSL1912530020080519 on April 6, 2022.

82   IBM. (n.d.). *The birth of the IBM PC.* Accessed at www.ibm.com /ibm/history/exhibits/pc25/pc25_birth.html on April 25, 2022.

83   Coca-Cola had only resumed production in China in 1981 after a thirty-three-year hiatus, and distribution was confined to the major cities.

84   Baark, E. (1990). China's software industry. *Information Technology for Development, 5*(2), 117–136. https://doi.org/10.1080/02681102.1 990.9627191

85   Wang, L., & Lewin, K. (2016). *Two decades of basic education in rural China.* Singapore: Springer.

86   Robertson, D., & Binis, J. B. (2022). *The cardboard classroom: A design-thinking guide for elementary teachers.* Bloomington, IN: Solution Tree Press, p. 2.

Chapter 4

87   Dartmouth Library. (n.d.). *Down to the Countryside Movement.* Accessed at www.library.dartmouth.edu/digital/digital -collections/down-countryside-movement on September 13, 2022.

88   Bonnin, M. (2013). *The lost generation: The rustication of China's educated youth (1968–1980)* (K. Horko, Trans.). Hong Kong: Chinese University Press. (Original work published in 2004)

89   Bonnin, M. (2013). *The lost generation: The rustication of China's educated youth (1968–1980)* (K. Horko, Trans.). Hong Kong: Chinese University Press. (Original work published in 2004)

90   Honig, E., & Zhao, X. (2015). Sent-down youth and rural economic development in Maoist China. *The China Quarterly, 222,* 499–521. https://doi.org/10.1017/S0305741015000363. See also: Chen, Y., Fan, Z., Gu, X., & Zhou, L. (2020). Arrival of young talent: The send-down movement and rural education in China. *American Economic Review, 110*(11), 3393–3430. https://doi.org/10.1257/aer.20191414

91   Vogel, E. F. (2011). *Deng Xiaoping and the transformation of China.* Cambridge, MA: Harvard University Press.

92   Vogel, E. F. (2011). *Deng Xiaoping and the transformation of China.* Cambridge, MA: Harvard University Press.

93   Cheng, A., & Wang, Q. (2012). English language teaching in higher education in China: A historical and social overview. In J. Ruan & C. B. Leung (Eds.), *Perspectives on teaching and learning English literacy in China* (pp. 19–33). Dordrecht, Netherlands: Springer.

94   Cheng, A., & Wang, Q. (2012). English language teaching in higher education in China: A historical and social overview. In J. Ruan & C. B. Leung (Eds.), *Perspectives on teaching and learning English literacy in China* (pp. 19–33). Dordrecht, Netherlands: Springer.

95   Harvey, D. (2005). *A brief history of neoliberalism.* Oxford, UK: Oxford University Press.

96   Vickers, E., & Xiaodong, Z. (2017). *Education and society in post-Mao China.* New York: Routledge.

97   Shenzhen was one of the first special economic zones and became a showcase for Deng's economic development policies. See also: Vogel, E. F. (2011). *Deng Xiaoping and the transformation of China.* Cambridge, MA: Harvard University Press.

98　Harter, S. (2012). *The construction of the self: Developmental and sociocultural foundations* (2nd ed.). New York: Guilford Press, p. 329.

99　Harter, S. (2012). *The construction of the self: Developmental and sociocultural foundations* (2nd ed.). New York: Guilford Press, p. 348.

100　Ho, D. Y. (1976). On the concept of face. *American Journal of Sociology, 81*(4), 867–884, p. 883.

101　Ho, D. Y. (1976). On the concept of face. *American Journal of Sociology, 81*(4), 867–884, p. 883.

102　University of Cambridge. (n.d.). *Student wellbeing.* Accessed at www.studentwellbeing.admin.cam.ac.uk/your-wellbeing/make -mistakes-and-learn-failure on April 7, 2022.

103　Grafwallner, P. (2021). *Not yet . . . and that's OK: How productive struggle fosters student learning.* Bloomington, IN: Solution Tree Press, p. 18.

104　This is commonly attributed to John Lennon but may have originated with Allen Saunders, a well-known writer, journalist, and cartoonist.

Chapter 5

105　To pacify the left wing of the CCP, in March 1979, Deng had declared the "four cardinal principles" to delineate the acceptable from the unacceptable in public expression: expressions should not question (1) the socialist path, (2) the dictatorship of the proletariat, (3) the Party leaders, or (4) Marxism–Leninism and Maoism. See also: Vogel, E. F. (2011). *Deng Xiaoping and the transformation of China.* Cambridge, MA: Harvard University Press.

106　Brick, A. B. (1990). *U.S. policy toward China a year after Tiananmen Square.* Accessed at www.policycommons.net/artifacts/1170518/ us/1723647/ on September 14, 2022.

107　Qiping, Y., & White, G. (1994). The "marketisation" of Chinese higher education: A critical assessment. *Comparative Education, 30*(3), 217–237.

108　Chen, L., & Huang, D. (2013). Internationalization of Chinese higher education. *Higher Education Studies, 3*(1), 92–105. http://dx.doi.org /10.5539/hes.v3n1p92

109　Vogel, E. F. (2011). *Deng Xiaoping and the transformation of China.* Cambridge, MA: Harvard University Press.

110 Vogel, E. F. (2011). *Deng Xiaoping and the transformation of China.* Cambridge, MA: Harvard University Press, pp. 576–577. Fang held status as an extraordinary astrophysicist who had entered Beijing University at age sixteen and later became the youngest full professor in China. Vogel notes that he exemplified the type of intellectual that Deng hoped to lure back to China. Many students lionized him and listened to and read his speeches.

111 Kwong, J. (1988). The 1986 student demonstrations in China: A democratic movement? *Asian Survey, 28*(9), 970–985. https://doi .org/10.2307/2644802

112 Plafker, T. (1997). China to stop assigning jobs to graduates. *Chronicle of Higher Education, 43*(23), A45.

113 Béja, J., & Goldman, M. (2009). The impact of the June 4th massacre on the pro-democracy movement. *China Perspectives, 2*, 18–28. https://doi.org/10.4000/chinaperspectives.4801

114 Béja, J. (Ed.). (2011). *The impact of China's 1989 Tiananmen massacre.* New York: Routledge.

115 Vogel, E. F. (2011). *Deng Xiaoping and the transformation of China.* Cambridge, MA: Harvard University Press.

116 Vogel, E. F. (2011). *Deng Xiaoping and the transformation of China.* Cambridge, MA: Harvard University Press.

117 The brutal suppression and forced assimilation of the Uyghur minority in Xinjiang, despite persistent foreign protests, attest to the relative ineffectiveness of this strategy.

118 Glăveanu, V. P. (2021). *The possible: A sociocultural theory.* New York: Oxford University Press, pp. 2–3.

119 Glăveanu, V. P. (2021). *The possible: A sociocultural theory.* New York: Oxford University Press, p. 3.

120 Glăveanu, V. P. (2021). *The possible: A sociocultural theory.* New York: Oxford University Press, p. 3.

Chapter 6

121 Vogel, E. F. (2011). *Deng Xiaoping and the transformation of China.* Cambridge, MA: Harvard University Press.

122 The Economist. (2021). *Why more young Chinese want to be civil
     servants.* Accessed at www.economist.com/china/2021/05/13/why
     -more-young-chinese-want-to-be-civil-servants on March 3, 2022.

123 Cuban, L. (1984). *How teachers taught: Constancy and change in
     American classrooms, 1890–1980.* New York: Longman.

124 Spence, J. D. (1996). *God's Chinese son: The Taiping heavenly kingdom
     of Hong Xiuquan.* New York: Norton.

125 Cziko, G. A. (1992). Purposeful behavior as the control of
     perception: Implications for educational research. *Educational
     Researcher, 21*(9), 10–27. https://doi.org/10.3102%2F001318
     9X021009010

126 Zhao, Y., & Cziko, G. A. (2001). Teacher adoption of technology:
     A perceptual control theory perspective. *Journal of Technology and
     Teacher Education, 9*(1), 5–30.

Chapter 7

127 Chivukula, R. S. (2016, September 19). *"There's a snake
     in the house!"* Accessed at https://undergrad.msu.edu/news/view
     /id/128 on April 8, 2022.

128 Bradford, P., Porciello, M., Balkon, N., & Backus, D. (2007). The
     Blackboard learning system: The be all and end all in educational
     instruction? *Journal of Educational Technology Systems, 35*(3),
     301–314. http://dx.doi.org/10.2190/X137-X73L-5261-5656

129 Green, P., Sha, M., & Liu, L. (2011). *The U.S.-China E-Language
     Project: A study of a gaming approach to English language learning for
     middle school students.* Accessed at www2.ed.gov/rschstat/eval/tech
     /us-china-e-language-project/report.pdf on March 4, 2022.

130 Green, P., Sha, M., & Liu, L. (2011). *The U.S.-China E-Language
     Project: A study of a gaming approach to English language learning for
     middle school students.* Accessed at www2.ed.gov/rschstat/eval/tech
     /us-china-e-language-project/report.pdf on March 4, 2022.

131 Bitar, S. (2004). *APEC International Seminar: The interaction between
     language, mathematics, science & ICT.* Accessed at www.apec
     .org/press/blogs/2004/0427_minsbitarintlseminar on March 4, 2022.

132 Zhao, Y. (2012). *World class learners: Educating creative and
     entrepreneurial students.* Thousand Oaks, CA: Corwin Press.

Chapter 8

133 Zhao, Y. (2009). *Catching up or leading the way: American education in the age of globalization*. Alexandria, VA: ASCD.

134 Tucker, M. S. (Ed.). (2011). *Surpassing Shanghai: An agenda for American education built on the world's leading systems*. Cambridge, MA: Harvard Education Press.

135 Jensen, B. (2012). *Catching up: Learning from the best school systems in East Asia*. Accessed at https://grattan.edu.au/report/catching-up -learning-from-the-best-school-systems-in-east-asia/ on March 3, 2022.

136 Loveless, T. (2019, December 19). *The children PISA ignores in China*. Accessed at www.brookings.edu/blog/brown-center -chalkboard/2019/12/19/the-children-pisa-ignores-in-china/?utm _source=pocket_mylist on March 3, 2022. According to this report, "In the 2018 PISA, only 4.9% of the tested students in B-S-J-Z lived in rural areas or villages with fewer than 3,000 people." *B-S-J-Z* stands for *Beijing-Shanghai-Jiangsu-Zhejiang*.

137 Kristof, N. (2011, January 15). China's winning schools? *The New York Times*. Accessed at www.nytimes.com/2011/01/16 /opinion/16kristof.html on March 3, 2022.

138 Bloomberg News. (2021, February 4). *China teaches school children 'do as President Xi tells you.'* Accessed at www.business-standard .com/article/international/china-teaches-school-children-do-as -president-xi-tells-you-121020401022_1.html on April 29, 2022.

139 European Commission Newsroom. (2021, June 4). *Bloomberg Innovation Index 2021*. Accessed at https://ec.europa.eu/newsroom /rtd/items/713430/en on March 4, 2022. According to the 2021 Bloomberg Innovation Index, this is no longer the case. The United States now lags behind several countries including Germany, South Korea, Singapore, and Switzerland. As is the case with test scores, this change may be less about the United States declining and more about other countries stepping up their game. Whether the Chinese governmental push for greater innovation and creativity is truly bearing fruit is difficult to determine. As a result of incentives and state investment, the number of patents filed and granted has increased tremendously between 2010–2020. It's not entirely clear how many of these represent true innovation.

140   Santacreu, A. M., & Zhu, H. (2018). *What does China's rise in patents mean? A look at quality vs. quantity.* Accessed at https://research .stlouisfed.org/publications/economic-synopses/2018/05/04/what -does-chinas-rise-in-patents-mean-a-look-at-quality-vs-quantity/ on March 4, 2022. An analysis of the data on Chinese patents between 2000–2016 concluded that "the actual technological improvement in China is not significant compared with its skyrocketing number of patent applications." The authors note that South Korea and China were catching up to Japan and the United States in patent quality.

141   Wininger, A. (2022). *Chinese invention patent and utility model grants both up 31% in 2021.* Accessed at www.natlawreview.com /article/chinese-invention-patent-and-utility-model-grants-both -31-2021 on March 4, 2022. Invention patents granted in China have increased significantly. In 2021, they were up 31 percent from 2020.

142   Stallings, J. (1980). Allocated academic learning time revisited, or beyond time on task. *Educational Researcher, 9*(11), 11–16. https:// doi.org/10.2307/1175185

143   Zhao, Y. (2014). *Who's afraid of the big bad dragon?* San Francisco: Jossey-Bass.

144   Gu, M., & Magaziner, J. (2016, May 2). The *gaokao*: History, reform, and rising international significance of China's national college entrance examination. *World Education News and Reviews.* Accessed at https://wenr.wes.org/2016/05/the-gaokao-history -reform-and-international-significance-of-chinas-national-college -entrance-examination on June 24, 2022.

145   Zhao, Y. (2009). *Catching up or leading the way: American education in the age of globalization.* Alexandria, VA: ASCD.

146   Bloomberg News. (2021, February 4). *China teaches school children 'do as President Xi tells you.'* Accessed at www.business-standard.com /article/international/china-teaches-school-children-do-as -president-xi-tells-you-121020401022_1.html on April 29, 2022.

147   No Child Left Behind (NCLB) Act of 2001, Pub. L. No. 107-110, § 115, Stat. 1425 (2002).

148   Race to the Top Act of 2011, H.R. 1532, 112th Congress (2011–2012).

149   McDiarmid, G. W., & Zhao, Y. (2022). *Learning for uncertainty: Teaching students how to thrive in a rapidly evolving world.* New York: Routledge.

150   Zhao, Y. (2018). *Reach for greatness: Personalizable education for all children.* Thousand Oaks, CA: Corwin.

151   Mooneyham, B., & Schooler, J. (2013). The costs and benefits of mind-wandering: A review. *Canadian Journal of Experimental Psychology, 67*(1), 11–18. https://doi.org/10.1037/a0031569

152   Isaacson, W. (2007). *Einstein: His life and universe.* New York: Simon & Schuster.

153   Zhao, Y. (2009). *Catching up or leading the way: American education in the age of globalization.* Alexandria, VA: ASCD, p. 61.

154   Zhao, Y. (2009). *Catching up or leading the way: American education in the age of globalization.* Alexandria, VA: ASCD, p. 59.

155   McDiarmid, G. W., & Zhao, Y. (2022). *Learning for uncertainty: Teaching students how to thrive in a rapidly evolving world.* New York: Routledge.

156   Hamilton, L., Stecher, B., Marsh, J., McCombs, J., Robyn, A., Russell, J., et al. (2007). *Standards-based accountability under No Child Left Behind: Experiences of teachers and administrators in three states.* Santa Monica, CA: RAND. Accessed at www.rand.org/pubs /monographs/MG589.html on September 20, 2022.

157   Tucker, M. S. (Ed.). (2011). *Surpassing Shanghai: An agenda for American education built on the world's leading systems.* Cambridge, MA: Harvard Education Press.

158   Zhao, Y. (2014). *Who's afraid of the big bad dragon?* San Francisco: Jossey-Bass. See also: Zhao, Y. (2020). Two decades of havoc: A synthesis of criticism against PISA. *Journal of Educational Change, 21,* 245–266. https://doi.org/10.1007/s10833-019-09367-x

159   McDiarmid, G. W., & Zhao, Y. (2022). *Learning for uncertainty: Teaching students how to thrive in a rapidly evolving world*. New York: Routledge. See also: Duckworth, A. (2016). *Grit: The power of passion and perseverance*. New York: Scribner. Levin, H. M. (2012). More than just test scores. *Prospects: The Quarterly Review of Comparative Education, 42*(3), 269–284. Panadero, E., Jonsson, A., & Botella, J. (2017). Effects of self-assessment on self-regulated learning and self-efficacy: Four meta-analyses. *Educational Research Review, 22*, 74–98. https://doi.org/10.1016/j.edurev.2017.08.004. Trilling, B., & Fadel, C. (2009). *21st century skills: Learning for life in our times*. San Francisco: Jossey-Bass. Wagner, T. (2008). *The global achievement gap: Why even our best schools don't teach the new survival skills our children need—And what we can do about it*. New York: Basic Books.

160   Hargreaves, A., & Shirley, D. (2009). *The fourth way: The inspiring future for educational change*. Thousand Oaks, CA: Corwin Press.

161   Komatsu, H., & Rappleye, J. (2017). A new global policy regime founded on invalid statistics? Hanushek, Woessmann, PISA, and economic growth. *Comparative Education, 53*(2), 166–191. https://doi.org/10.1080/03050068.2017.1300008. See also: Zhao, Y. (2020). Two decades of havoc: A synthesis of criticism against PISA. *Journal of Educational Change, 21*, 245–266. https://doi.org/10.1007/s10833-019-09367-x

162   IATED. (2020, March 20). *Yong Zhao—Reach for greatness: Personalizable education for all—INTED2020 keynote speech* [Video file]. Accessed at www.youtube.com/watch?v=CvqCfgHVLGs on March 4, 2022.

163   Zhao, Y. (2018). *Reach for greatness: Personalizable education for all children*. Thousand Oaks, CA: Corwin.

164   Wehmeyer, M., & Zhao, Y. (2020). *Teaching students to become self-determined learners*. Alexandria, VA: ASCD.

165   Zhao, Y., Zhang, G., Lei, J., & Qiu, W. (2016). *Never send a human to do a machine's job: Correcting the top 5 edtech mistakes*. Thousand Oaks, CA: Corwin.

166   Zhao, Y. (2015, October 26). *Never send a human to do a machine's job: Top 5 mistakes in ed tech* [Blog post]. Accessed at https://nepc.colorado.edu/blog/never-send on March 4, 2022.

167   McDiarmid, G. W., & Zhao, Y. (2022). *Learning for uncertainty: Teaching students how to thrive in a rapidly evolving world.* New York: Routledge.

168   Zhao, Y., & Gearin, B. (Eds.). (2018). *Imagining the future of global education: Dreams and nightmares.* New York: Routledge. See also: Zhao, Y., Tavangar, H., McCarren, E., Rshaid, G., & Tucker, K. (2016). *Schools as global enterprises.* Thousand Oaks, CA: Corwin.

169   Bloomberg News. (2021, February 4). *China teaches school children 'do as President Xi tells you.'* Accessed at www.business-standard .com/article/international/china-teaches-school-children-do-as -president-xi-tells-you-121020401022_1.html on April 29, 2022.

170   Leonhardt, D. (2022, May 5). 'Not good for learning': New research is showing the high costs of long school closures in some communities. *The New York Times.* Accessed at www.nytimes .com/2022/05/05/briefing/school-closures-covid-learning-loss.html on June 24, 2022.

171   Christopher, E. (2022). Teachers are tired (that's why they need our support now more than ever). Ed., 44–51. Accessed at www.gse .harvard.edu/sites/default/files/edmag/pdfs/2022-SUM.pdf on September 20, 2022.

172   Lloyd, G. E. R. (2007). *Cognitive variations: Reflections on the unity and diversity of the human mind.* Oxford, UK: Clarendon Press, p. 175.

173   McDiarmid, G. W., & Zhao, Y. (2022). *Learning for uncertainty: Teaching students how to thrive in a rapidly evolving world.* New York: Routledge.

174   National Association of Independent Schools. (2021, June 14). *Yong Zhao: The future of education* [Video file]. Accessed at www.youtube .com/watch?v=Kjdymx8MTHY on September 20, 2022.

Epilogue

175   Sun, J., Dunne, M., Hou, X., & Xu, A. (2013). Educational stress among Chinese adolescents: Individual, family, school and peer influences. *Educational Review, 65*(3), 284–302. https://doi.org/10.10 80/00131911.2012.659657

176   Guisbond, L. (2012). *NCLB's lost decade for educational progress: What can we learn from this policy failure?* Accessed at https://files .eric.ed.gov/fulltext/ED529798.pdf on March 4, 2022.

177   McDiarmid, G. W., & Zhao, Y. (2022). *Learning for uncertainty: Teaching students how to thrive in a rapidly evolving world.* New York: Routledge.

178   Freud, S. (1950). *The interpretation of dreams* (A. A. Brill, Trans.). New York: Modern Library.

179   Hofstadter, R. (1963). *Anti-intellectualism in American life.* New York: Knopf.

180   van der Post, L. (1958). *The lost world of the Kalahari.* New York: Morrow.

Index

middle school. *See also* education, access to
  academic success and, 36–37
  anti-authoritarian and, 41–42
Milton, D., 34
Mindful School Communities (Mason, Murphy, and Jackson), 27–28
Ming, G.
  access to education, 33
  environmental factors, 6
  example of, 13–14, 20
  reflections on, 26
  rule-breaking, 25
  an unconventional father, 15–16
modernization, 85–86
Mormonism, 107–109
Murphy, M., 27–28

N

neoliberalism, 71, 152, 156, 157
neuroticism, 9
New York, Colgate University and Hamilton College in, 124–129
Nicolaou, N., 8
No Child Left Behind (NCLB) Act, 148, 163
non-cognitive skills, 152
Not Yet . . . And That's OK (Grafwallner), 80

O

openness, 9
opportunity, influence of personality and, 7–9
optimism, 8
Oregon
  Linfield College, 91, 92, 98–100, 101–106, 115
  University of Oregon, 135–136
  Willamette University, 124, 125

P

pedagogy
  comparing Chinese and Western pedagogy, 102–104
  higher education, 54–55
Pepper, S., 32–33
perceptual control theory (PCT), 113
personality, influence of, 7–9
personalized education for all students, 153–154
Peterson, P., 119–121, 131
Pluchino, A., 1
possibilities, the, 94, 95, 140
poverty, 17–20, 26
private sector jobs, 103
probabilities for the future, xv–xviii
professorship
  AERA submissions platform, 119–121, 131–133
  big questions, 135–138
  computer clubhouse project, 129–131
  cultural identity, 138–139
  international connections, 133–134
  reflections on, 139–142
  software development, 124–129
  temporary jobs, 122–124
Programme for International Student Assessment (PISA). *See also* assessments
  danger of, 152–153
  high-stakes assessment and, 151–153

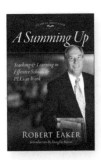

A Summing Up
Robert Eaker
After a career spanning nearly half a century, Robert Eaker delivers a work of reflection and storytelling. Learn from a master educator as he shares the story of his career, along with in-depth guidance for implementing the Professional Learning Community at Work® process.
BKF943

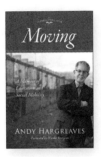

Moving
Andy Hargreaves
Social mobility—the chance, through education, to achieve greater success than one's parents—is a compelling issue of our time. Beginning in 1950s Northern England, this revealing memoir links Andy Hargreaves's experiences of social mobility to today's challenges of inequity and immobility.
BKF953

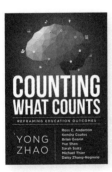

Counting What Counts
Edited by Yong Zhao
Essential traits such as mindset, motivation, social skills, creativity, and entrepreneurial spirit need to be acknowledged and cultivated in the classroom. Educators must shift the evaluation paradigm to focus on a multiplicity of skills necessary for success in the 21st century.
BKF632

Deeper Learning
Edited by James A. Bellanca
Education authorities from around the globe draw on research as well as their own experience to explore deeper learning, a process that promotes higher-order thinking, reasoning, and problem solving to better educate students and prepare them for college and careers.
BKF622